YORK BUSINES

GENERAL EDITOR:
Sir Kenneth Alexander

MICROECONOMICS

Ronald Shone

B.Sc. (ECON) (HULL), M.A. (ESSEX)
Senior lecturer in Economics, University of Stirling

LONGMAN
YORK PRESS

YORK PRESS
Immeuble Esseily, Place Riad Solh, Beirut.

LONGMAN GROUP UK LIMITED
Longman House,
Burnt Mill,
Harlow,
Essex.

© Librairie du Liban 1987

First published 1987
ISBN 0 582 00345 8
Printed in Singapore

Contents

Chapter 1

Introduction and markets

What is microeconomics?

Economics is the study of how countries use their limited resources, such as land, labour and natural resources to produce goods and services and to provide for the wants of their members. It attempts to answer a number of important questions, such as:

(1) What allows a country to produce goods and services in increasing quantities?
(2) Can all demands be satisfied?
(3) Does the distribution of income make any difference to growth?
(4) Should governments intervene in the economic system?
(5) What determines the price of commodities and natural resources?
(6) Is international trade beneficial?
(7) What determines the output at which a firm produces?

These are just some of the questions. Economics is accordingly a very broad subject and so it is common to break it down. The first major division is into microeconomics and macroeconomics.

Microeconomics is concerned with *individual decision units*, such as a person, a single market, a firm, or a single commodity. Macroeconomics, however, deals with the economy as a whole and is concerned with characteristics of the whole economy, such as the economy's rate of growth, the rate of unemployment and inflation, government spending and the demand for and supply of money.

A particular problem can be both microeconomic and macroeconomic depending on how it is approached. Consider subsidising grain. (A *subsidy* is where the government, or some organization, pays the grain producer an amount of money so that the grain producer can sell the grain at a lower price.) We can investigate at the microeconomic level the effect of such a subsidy on the price of grain, on the quantity purchased and on the distribution of income. This is part of microeconomics. But suppose we wish to consider *all* subsidies provided by the government and wish to consider in what way the government obtains money to pay for these subsidies. This is part of macroeconomics. Because in microeconomics we limit our study to just one (or a few) decision units we are not concerned about the impact at the broader level. When we consider a subsidy on grain our attention is directed at the effects this has on price, sales and distribution. We do not consider where the money came from.

Where the money came from and whether it is sufficient is part of macroeconomics.

Microeconomics does not deal only with individual decision units; it is also concerned with how resources are allocated within an economy so as to produce the goods and services that people want. Microeconomics is also concerned with whether the allocation of goods and services is done efficiently (which, for the moment, can be taken to mean in the cheapest possible way).

Markets

In dealing with *how* resources are allocated, an important feature of this is the type of *market* which is involved. A market is simply where those who supply something can interact with those who wish to demand it. The local market is the simplest example. Here people come together, some to sell and others to buy. Not only commodities, such as grain or honey, are bought and sold, but also services such as cleaning shoes or having a haircut. As we move further away from the local market we can consider the market for labour. Firms demand labour services while people supply labour services. A market for labour is not in a well defined locality – as is the local food market – but it is a market in the economic sense because it brings together buyers and sellers. In the same way, there is a market for foreign exchange. There are people buying foreign currency and others selling it. The market may be world wide; or, in the case where currency restrictions occur, in the 'black' market. Some markets, like those for foreign exchange and oil, are international. Buyers occur in a number of countries and sellers also belong to a number of countries. But all markets have in common the fact that buyers and sellers are brought together – whether physically or over the telephone and telex system.

Markets, then, have buyers which give rise to a demand for the good or service and sellers which give rise to the supply of this good or service. As we shall see later, demand and supply interact to determine the price at which commodities and services are bought and sold. But it is important to be clear that markets are part of the *economic system*, and how they operate in practice depends on which type of economic system is in existence.

Economic systems

What do we mean by an economic system and how many systems are there? We pointed out that microeconomics is concerned with individual decision units – like firms and households. The economic system includes households, firms and the government (or the state). We can think of the government as including all the main institutions – such as the tax collecting institution, the Central Bank and other state run organizations. The economic system in simple terms is composed of these three groups of decision units: households, firms and the state. The type of economic system which prevails depends on where in the economic system decisions are actually made.

The command economy

Consider an extreme case where the state makes all decisions. This is referred to as a command economy. Although no such economy exists in practice it does highlight the features of economies where many decisions are made by the state. The situation can be seen in terms of Fig. 1. Firms are represented at the top and households at the bottom. The state is the centre of the economic system. The arrows show decisions. Since the arrows all go from the state in the centre, this indicates that the state decides which firms produce what commodities (or services) and how much to produce. The state also decides what households can consume and how much they can consume.

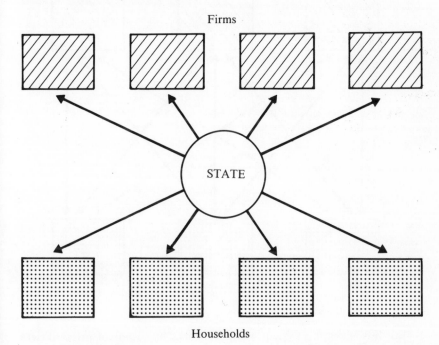

FIG. 1: **Command economy**

In this command economy all decisions are made by the state and there is no need for buyers to come together with sellers. All allocation is done by the state. To the extent that people may want more of a commodity than the state is allowing firms to produce, then households must be rationed. If firms want more steel than the state is allowing to be produced or imported, then steel must be rationed.

The market economy

A second type of economic system is the market economy. This is the other extreme from the command economy. In this type of system, firms and households come together by means of markets to decide what to produce, for whom to produce and how much to produce. All decisions are made by individual households and individual firms. This market economy is represented in Fig. 2. Notice that each arrow has two heads and all households interact with all firms. The state plays almost no role – except to preserve health and safety.

Firms

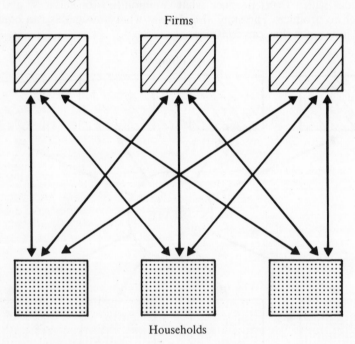

Households

FIG. 2: **Market economy**

But how does this system work? It works by means of prices. Prices operate as signals. A seller will be prepared to sell more at a higher price while a buyer will buy less at a higher price (as we shall see later). If the price is too high then a seller will not be able to sell all he would wish. There will then be unsold items. This is a signal to lower the price. If the price is too low then a seller will sell all his goods very quickly indeed.

This is a signal that he could have still sold all his goods, but probably at a higher price. It is a signal for him to raise his price.

Both the command economy and the market economy perform the same task: to decide who produces what, for whom and how much. In fact, whatever the economic system it must deal with these three aspects: what to produce, for whom to produce and how much to produce. The market economy does not require an elaborate state machinery to make these decisions. The price will give constant signals to buyers and sellers to adjust their demands and supplies. If there is no state involvement in markets at all, this is sometimes referred to as a free market economy. Decision makers are free to make their individual decisions without any state involvement.

Problems of command and market economies

These two extreme forms of economic systems have a number of supporters. Although no economy operates exactly like those just described, the USSR and China come closest to the command economy while the USA comes closest to the market economy. Supporters of the free market system point out problems with the command economy, while supporters of the planning system point out problems with the market economy. What briefly are these problems?

For the command economy the most obvious problem is to obtain information on all commodities and see that different decisions are not inconsistent. For instance, that its decisions on the number of cars to allow households is matched by consistent decisions on steel and other materials to firms so that they can produce this number of cars. It is no good allowing households to purchase 1000 cars when only 750 can be produced! Since the economic system is inter-dependent (steel is used to produce van bodies and the vans are used to deliver foodstuffs, etc.) then this requires not only a great deal of information, but also technical skill in ensuring that the decisions are not inconsistent.

A command economy does not allow individuals to contribute in any way to decisions. Whatever their ability, they must accept the state decisions. Such a restriction on individual liberty leads to tensions in society. Of course, it is possible to allow *some* individual decisions so that the economic system allows individual initiative by giving some individual incentives. This has certainly taken place in the USSR and China, but this moves us away from the command economy. It is a recognition that a *pure* command economy is not a practical system.

There is a third difficulty which is that individual groups or firms may try to bring pressure to bear on the state planners to have their wants met. This can quickly lead to bribery and black markets.

The free market economy has problems also. For a free market economy to operate, property must be in private hands. Farmers own the land and businessmen own factories. They hire labour services and purchase other materials to produce and through the sale of such products make profits. If they make bad decisions then they may make losses or less profits than they could have made. The profit is seen in such a system as the reward for undertaking such decisions, coping with uncertainty, risk and changing market conditions. It is assumed that if bad decisions are made repeatedly then a business will make repeated losses and will soon cease production all together.

But large profits may arise simply from being a large organization which is powerful enough to fight off competition and powerful enough to charge a high price for what it produces. The point here is whether consumers' wants are being satisfied by producers, or whether a few producers are supplying a restricted set of commodities which households must choose to purchase or purchase something totally different. For example, a large organization may wish to produce commodity x. It may engage in a large advertising campaign to convince households that they ought to purchase x. This means, if they are successful, that firms do not produce to satisfy consumer wants but rather create consumer wants to match with what they themselves wish to supply.

Some goods have external effects which are not taken account of in the market mechanism. Suppose for example, a large chemical plant is set up just on the edge of town. The firm is using labour and other material inputs in order to produce chemicals which allows it to make profits. But suppose the chemical waste leads to poor health of the people in the town. The firm does not take account of this in its decision-making because the effect is *external* to the firm. But it is a cost to society. In fact, much pollution caused by firms is external to the firm in the sense that society must bear the cost of the pollution rather than the firm creating it. We shall deal with this topic more fully in Chapter 12.

Is there a market for health? Many people will benefit from improved health. But health is very costly to provide – so costly in fact that no one firm could provide it. There is a want which cannot be provided by individual firms. It is possible, in such circumstances, for the state to provide a health service and use taxes to cover the cost of such a service. Some services are essential: refuse disposal; sewage treatment and disposal; the provision of clean drinking water. The absence of these services would lead to epidemics, which, as well as the suffering to individuals and families caused by illnesses would have adverse effects on the economy of the state. Of course, it is possible for *some* specific health problems to be privately supplied (e.g., dental care or minor operations) but the point is that not *all* health can be so supplied. The same is true for education and law and order.

Another problem with the market mechanism is that it may lead to too high a price for, say, a staple commodity. Suppose the market for grain was totally free. It is possible for the market price to be such that a large proportion of the population cannot pay such a price and so suffer from starvation. The state may then decide that on moral grounds it should set a price for grain below the market price by subsidising grain production (we shall deal with this later). In other situations the government may tax companies in order to cover the cost which society has to bear from any externality – as in the chemical firm discussed above.

We see therefore, that both the command economy and the market economy have problems. The command economy can be relaxed by allowing more individual decisions so that incentives can be incorporated into the system; while in the market economy the system can be changed by allowing the state to operate in some form in some of the markets. We arrive, then, at a *mixed economy*. How mixed depends on whether the majority (but not all) of decisions lie with the state or whether the majority (but not all) of decisions lie with households and firms.

Plan of the book

Markets bring together buyers and sellers. The main buyers are households and their wants give rise to the demand for various commodities. In Chapter 2 we look more closely at consumer wants and in Chapter 3 we consider how these wants get transferred into demands. Having considered demand we then consider what determines the supply of goods and services, which we do in Chapters 4 and 5. Demand and supply are the main tools of analysis for analysing how markets work. Chapter 6 provides some typical situations. However, when we consider more deeply how prices are determined we find that it depends on the type of competition that firms are involved in. At one extreme we have *perfect competition* which involves many sellers, none of which can determine the price. This we deal with in Chapter 7. At the other extreme we have a *monopoly*, where a commodity is provided by only one seller. Being the only firm to supply this commodity he will have much more control over the price – exactly how, we shall consider in Chapter 8. Most market conditions fall between these two extremes and involve a relatively small number of firms competing with each other, and this we refer to as *oligopoly* (meaning a few sellers). There are many varieties of oligopoly depending on the type of competition we assume, and in Chapter 9 we shall consider just some of these.

Firms require labour and raw materials to produce commodities. Even a service requires labour and time. Such inputs are grouped into three broad categories: land, labour and capital. Whatever commodity or service that is produced or supplied, it requires some or all of land, labour and capital. Land, labour and capital are referred to as *factors of production*. In Chapter 10 we shall consider the demand for and supply of just one factor input, namely labour.

One of the main concerns of economics is whether a firm is efficient or whether a market is operating efficiently. In Chapter 11 we shall see more fully what economists means when they talk of 'efficiency'.

Throughout Chapters 2–10 we will be dealing largely with markets that operate freely. In Chapter 12 we consider how governments involve themselves in markets and what influences they can have on price, demand and supply. We have left this to the end because, in general, government involvement in the economic system adapts the market mechanism but does not replace it. In other words, decisions still lie with households and firms but now the government may place additional constraints on those choices, e.g. they may set a maximum price for grain or establish for producers the price at which oil will sell on world markets.

The book concludes with a series of questions the reader can consider to see if he has understood the discussion.

Since economics has quite a number of technical words and phrases, a glossary is provided at the end of the book. Where a word or phrase *first occurs* in the book it is explained.

Chapter 2

Consumer choice

Scarcity and choice

In this chapter and the next we shall consider how an individual chooses between commodities and what constrains this choice. All consumers have many wants but not all these wants can be satisfied. However, the fact that wants are many and resources are limited is not restricted to the individual. An employer too would want a number of inputs, such as labour and capital, but he is restricted by the cost he has to pay for them. Even governments would like to undertake many projects but are limited by the funds that they can raise in taxes or by borrowing. The simple fact is that wants are many, resources are scarce and so a choice must be made. *Scarcity and choice* are at the very foundation of microeconomics.

Consider a situation where you have an evening to do something with. You may have the possibility of going to the cinema, going to a show, or simply staying at home. The point is that doing one prevents you from doing the other. Your time is a limitation on what you *can* do. You may *wish* to go to the cinema and to the show. But that is not possible. You must make a *choice*. Even millionaires must make choices. Although the very rich have little or no restriction on what they can afford to purchase, they must still make choices. A trip by a millionaire to London or New York means he cannot be elsewhere. He must choose whether he wishes to make the trip or not. Obviously he can afford it, but the question is whether he wishes to use his income *and* his time in this way.

For most individuals, income is the main limitation on what they can choose. We all want plenty of food, clothing, shelter and other items that make our living comfortable and satisfying. However, the income we have means that we cannot satisfy all these wants. We must make a choice. It is important, therefore, to distinguish wants from demand. *A want becomes a demand only when it is backed by the ability to pay.* You may want a car but if you do not have the ability to pay for it then this is not a demand for a car: it is simply a want (a wish). If you want a car and have the income to purchase it, then this want becomes a demand for a car. This is a vital point which is important in understanding how the market mechanism works. The very poor may want bread, but if they do not have the income to purchase such bread, then these desires remain as wants and do not get translated into demand. When an economist talks of demand, he means wants which are backed by the ability to pay.

If we consider the market for bread, say, then we can add up individual demands for bread and arrive at the total demand. The characteristics of this total demand we shall consider in detail in the next chapter.

Wants: total and marginal utility

Everyone has wants. Consider your own wants. These will include a place to sleep, food to eat, clothes to keep you warm. These are basic wants. But then there are less basic wants. Pens to write with, paper to write on, radios and television sets, a bicycle or car, and so on. Wants are unlimited. Even the richest individual still has some wants which he would like to be satisfied. The important point is that we order our wants from the most important to the the least important. You would rate as important food, clothing and a place to live. These wants are top of the list. Only when these wants have been partially satisfied do you consider other wants. But even basic wants can be satisified in a variety of ways. You may want food, but this can be satisfied either by means of bread or by means of meat. Which do you choose? This is what this chapter is about: on what basis you choose to satisfy your variety of wants. But for the moment let us continue to discuss wants.

You want bread, a bicycle and clothes because these commodities give satisfaction. In other words, when a commodity fulfils a want then you receive satisfaction. Economists have a phrase for this and say that you receive *utility* (another word for satisfaction) from commodities. This utility arises because your wants are being fulfilled. Thus you get utility from bread, from a bicycle and from clothes.

Utility is a rather difficult concept. You know that you get satisfaction from bread and you may be able to tell me whether you get more, less or the same satisfaction from meat as from bread. But you cannot tell me by how much more or how much less satisfaction. You cannot measure utility or satisfaction. But even so, we can say a number of things which are very important.

Suppose you have just finished eating some bread which you enjoyed. I now give you a second piece of bread which you eat. It too gives you satisfaction (utility) but possibly not quite as much as the first. Certainly the third piece of bread I give you does not give you as much satisfaction as the first or possibly the second. What is being experienced is a decline in the satisfaction arising from each additional unit. Of course, your total utility is rising because each piece of bread gives you some positive additional utility, but the additional amount is declining. This change in the total utility with each additional unit is so important that economists give it a name: they call it *marginal utility*. (Marginal just means a little more or a little less, and we shall be using the term at various places throughout this book.)

We have just noticed that as you consume more, the additional utility you get from each additional unit declines: that is, marginal utility declines with each extra unit consumed. Notice that we do not need to have a precise measure of utility to know that marginal utility is declining when you increase your consumption. Also note that if you reduce your consumption by one unit, the marginal utility rises.

Now suppose you wanted to get the maximum satisfaction from eating loaves of bread, assuming they are free. How many would you eat? You eat the first, second and third, say. Each is giving satisfaction but we know that the additional satisfaction is declining. So long as the marginal

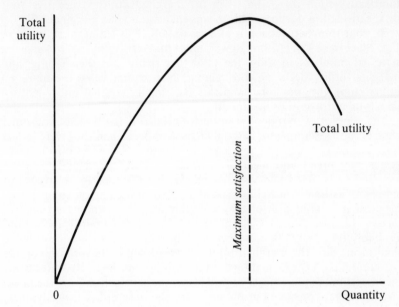

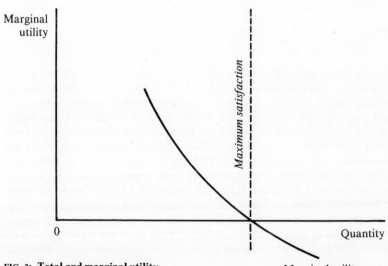

FIG. 3: **Total and marginal utility**

utility is positive then you can continue to increase your total satisfaction (your total utility). When the marginal utility is negative what does this mean? It means that the extra loaf of bread *reduced* your total satisfaction. We see, then, that when the marginal utility is positive your total satisfaction rises, and when the marginal utility is negative your total satisfaction declines. This means that when your marginal utility is zero, your total satisfaction is at a maximum. This situation is drawn in Fig. 3 (see page 15). (Although we cannot measure utility, we can give it a series of numbers to show the total first rising and then falling, and marginal utility declining throughout.) Notice that when the marginal utility curve cuts the horizontal axis (i.e. when marginal utility is zero) then total utility is at its maximum.

The concept of marginal utility just outlined is the basis of consumer choice. In the example we had only loaves of bread and they were in fact free. The only choice was how many to consume. Consider now just two goods, say bread and meat. The prices of both bread and meat are assumed to be fixed and your income is also assumed to be fixed. For simplicity assume you were to spend all of your income on either bread, meat, or a combination of the two. Now imagine spending all of your income on just bread. Will this give you the maximum satisfaction? Probably not. Why? Because you are consuming relatively more bread than meat, then the marginal utility of bread will be low. Since you are consuming no meat its marginal utility will be very high. By transferring income from bread to meat you will lose some satisfaction from the bread you no longer consume but obtain relatively more utility from the meat you do consume. When will you stop switching from bread to meat? When the last unit of income transferred to meat gives the same satisfaction as the last unit of bread given up. This can be stated as follows:

$$\frac{\text{marginal utility of bread}}{\text{price of bread}} = \frac{\text{marginal utility of meat}}{\text{price of meat}}$$

Notice that each marginal utility is divided by the price of the commodity. This is because the last unit in each case has to be bought at a different price. We can now see what is happening. If you consume only bread then the left hand side will be low relative to the right hand side whatever the respective prices of the commodities. As you switch your income from bread to meat then the marginal utility of bread *rises* (because you are consuming less) and the marginal utility of meat falls (because you are consuming more). At some combination of bread and meat the two will be equal. Had you continued to consume more meat and less bread then the left hand side would be greater than the right hand side. Then it would be better to switch out of meat and into bread. Your satisfaction will be maximised when both sides are equal. Only then will you not benefit from switching from one commodity and into the other.

From this result we can now see what happens when the price changes. Suppose the consumer is maximising his utility and the condition above holds. We then say the consumer is in *equilibrium*. The consumer will remain in this position until something changes. Now suppose there is a plentiful supply of bread and the price of bread falls. What will the consumer do? If the price of bread falls, then at the original quantities being purchased, the left hand side will now be greater than the right hand side. The individual can therefore increase his utility by transferring out of meat and into bread. This will lower the marginal utility of bread (because he is now consuming more) and raise the marginal utility of meat (since he is now consuming less). He will stop purchasing extra bread when both sides are equal.

We have *explained*, then, why when the price of bread falls a person will buy more. This is true of almost all commodities. The reason lies in the characteristic that the marginal utility falls when more is consumed.

To ensure you have fully understood this, try to reason out, before reading on, why less meat is bought when the price rises. It is because as the price rises the right hand side falls and so the consumer will obtain more satisfaction by moving out of meat and into bread. Consequently, demand falls when the price rises.

The margin versus the total

In the last section we talked about total satisfaction (total utility) and the extra satisfaction (marginal utility) from consuming more. There is a direct relationship between total and marginal, which occurs throughout microeconomics, and so it is worth considering it further. But we have a problem. We cannot measure utility. Just so that we can see the relationship between total and marginal let us suppose we can measure utility precisely (remembering that the results so far do not require this to be so). Let us call the unit of measurement 'utils'. Now consider what is happening to a person's satisfaction as he consumes more and more of, say, bread. The information is presented in Table 1.

TABLE 1: **Total and marginal utility**

Number of loaves of bread	Total utility (utils)	Marginal utility (utils)
1	100	—
2	180	80
3	255	75
4	315	60
5	345	30
6	345	0
7	330	−15

This table shows a number of the features that we have discussed so far. First, however, how do we obtain marginal utility? Since the marginal utility is the extra utility from consuming an extra unit, we obtain the first figure by subtracting the total utility of consuming 1 loaf of bread (100 utils) from that obtained from consuming 2 loaves of bread (180 utils), giving a marginal utility of 80 utils. And so on down the table. Notice that the marginal utility of bread falls as the person consumes more. Second, the total utility is at maximum when the marginal utility is zero (it reaches 345 utils when 6 loaves of bread are consumed). Third, when the marginal utility is negative then total utility declines. Table 1, therefore, verifies what we drew in Fig. 3.

Let us now include money. Money also has a marginal utility and the price of money is taken to be unity (i.e., one). Thus we have an equilibrium for a consumer when:

$$\frac{\text{marginal utility of bread}}{\text{price of bread}} = \text{marginal utility of money}$$

Suppose the marginal utility of money is constant at 6 utils for \$1. Now how many loaves of bread will this person purchase if the price of bread were \$10? We have:

$$\frac{\text{marginal utility of bread}}{10} = \frac{6}{1}$$

Hence:

marginal utility of bread $= 10 \times 6 = 60$ utils.

He will accordingly purchase 4 loaves of bread. If he purchased only 3 loaves of bread his marginal utility from the third loaf would be 75 utils, while holding money gives only 60 utils. It is worth his while, then, exchanging money for bread.

What happens when the price of bread rises to \$12½? Then we have that the marginal utility of bread must equal $12½ \times 6 = 75$ utils. He will accordingly purchase 3 loaves of bread and not 4.

The water–diamond paradox

The distinction between total and marginal utility explains a famous paradox. The paradox, framed as a question, is this:

Why, when water is so important for life, is it so cheap in most countries: and diamonds, which are not necessary for life, have a high value?

This paradox allows us to make a number of important points while trying to explain it. The first point is that the word 'value' has more than one meaning. There is value in *use* and value in *exchange*. When you purchase something you do so because it gives you satisfaction. It is useful to you because it fulfils a want. This use value is referring to the *total* satisfaction or total utility you derive from *all the units* that you consume. The value in exchange, however, is reflecting what the *last* unit was valued at to you. In other words, the value in exchange is referring to the marginal utility derived from the last unit purchased.

We saw this above. The exchange value is reflected in the price, and when loaves of bread were priced at $10 you purchased 4 because at this price the value to you of the fourth loaf of bread (60 utils) just equalled the value of money you paid *in exchange*. Consequently, value in use refers to total utility while value in exchange refers to marginal utility.

The paradox is now easy to resolve. When referring to water the paradox is indicating that water has a very high total utility but a very low marginal utility. Because the marginal utility of water is low so is the price. Diamonds, on the other hand, have a rather low total utility but a very high marginal utility. Because the marginal utility of diamonds is high so is the price.

If you find this paradox difficult, another example may help to clarify the points made. Consider a prisoner of war camp in which there is no money, but cigarettes are being used to exchange for other goods (soap, razor blades, food, etc.). Consider two prisoners, one who smokes and the other who does not. To the prisoner who smokes, cigarettes have *two* features. They give satisfaction (value in use) and they can be used to purchase other items (value in exchange). To the non-smoker they simply have value in exchange. In fact, whenever something can be used also as a medium of exchange then it has both a value in use and a value in exchange. Gold is by far the most usual commodity which has both a value in use (as ornamentation, in dentistry, and in some industrial processes) and value in exchange (in the form of gold coins or gold bars).

Chapter 3

Demand

IN THE PREVIOUS CHAPTER we demonstrated that as the price of a commodity rose a person consumed less of it. Because a person consumed less he would accordingly demand less of that commodity. This is a fundamental result of market forces: demand falls when the price rises and demand rises when the price falls. Since this is true for almost all individuals (the few exceptions we can ignore) then the demand for, say, bread by all households follows the same pattern.

We can display this result in either of two ways: as a table or by means of a graph. In Table 2 we have the different demands for bread at different prices. The same information is displayed in Fig. 4 on page 21.

TABLE 2: **Demand schedule**

Price (p)	Quantity (q)
1	55
2	50
3	45
4	40
5	35
6	30
7	25
8	20

The only difference is that we have joined up all the points to form a curve. This is called a *demand curve*, and is denoted "D". It is common to draw the demand curve with price on the vertical axis and the quantity demanded on the horizontal axis. A demand curve, then, shows the relationship between the price of a commodity and the quantity of that commodity as the price varies. It is important to be clear that we are assuming nothing else changes. Thus, if the price rises from $3 to $4, and only the price, then the quantity demanded will fall from 45 to 40.

Although we realize the demand for a commodity depends on many things besides the price of that commodity, this particular relationship is very important if we wish to know how prices are determined in the market. As we pointed out in Chapter 1, the price is a signal both to demanders and suppliers. Here we are dealing only with it as a signal to demanders.

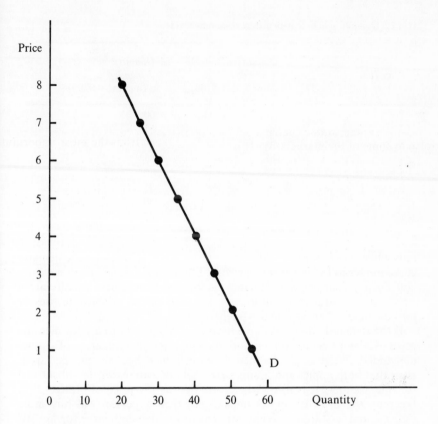

FIG. 4: **Demand curve**

What else determines a person's demand for a commodity? Another important determinant is a person's level of income. Generally, the greater your level of income the more you can purchase of a good. The normal situation is one where as your income rises you demand more of a commodity. When this occurs the good is referred to as a *normal good*. What happens to the demand curve in Fig. 4 when income rises, say from $100 to $200? We again supply the information in both a table and a graph. What we see from both Table 3 and Fig. 5 (see pages 22 and 23) is that for each price, the quantity demanded is greater at the higher level of income. The demand curve moves to the right from D_1 to D_2. If this is true for almost all households, then for households as a whole the market demand curve also moves to the right for a rise in income.

But this is not the only result of income changes. For some commodities, as income rises you replace these with alternative (possibly better quality) commodities. If this happens, then as income rises the quantity demanded will actually *fall*. A good whose quantity demanded

TABLE 3: **Demand schedule with different income levels**

Price (p)	Quantity demanded q (income = $100)	Quantity demanded q (income = $200)
1	55	60
2	50	55
3	45	50
4	40	45
5	35	40
6	30	35
7	25	30
8	20	25

falls when income rises is called an *inferior good*. In this case the demand curve moves to the *left* as income *rises*. For another range of commodities you do not change your demands as income rises. These usually are a small part of your expenditure, e.g. salt and spices. As income rises or falls the demand curve remains unchanged.

If the demand curves we have been discussing refer to apples then the price is the price of apples and the quantity the quantity of apples demanded. What might happen if oranges now become cheaper? It is clear that both apples and oranges are fruit and can readily be substituted for one another. It is likely, therefore, that as the price of oranges falls (keeping the price of apples unchanged) then a person will buy more oranges and less apples. What happens to the demand curve for apples? No matter what the price of apples happens to be, if the price of oranges falls then *less* apples will be demanded. This means that the demand curve for apples moves to the *left*. This is a general result. If the price of a *substitute* commodity falls then the demand for the other commodity also falls (i.e. the demand curve moves to the left). The more substitutable commodities are (e.g. bread and rice may be considered more substitutable than bread and clothes) then the greater will be the movement of the demand for one commodity as the price of the substitute commodity changes.

Some commodities are demanded together, e.g. knives and forks, transistor radio and ear phones. When the price of one falls (e.g. transistor radios) the demand for it rises. But because the two commodities are used together, the demand for the other (ear phones) also rises. These commodities are said to be *complements*. Thus, when the price of a commodity falls, the demand for the complementary commodity rises. This increase in the demand for the complementary commodity gives rise to a shift in its demand curve because we are *not* dealing with a change in its price (which would reflect a movement along the demand curve), but

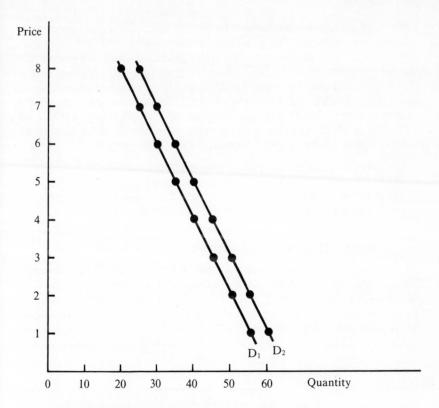

FIG. 5: **Change in demand arising from a rise in income**

rather a change in something which was previously held constant when drawing the demand curve (namely, the price of the other good). Hence, the demand curve shifts to the right for a fall in the price of a complementary commodity.

One final factor shifts the demand curve for a commodity: namely, a change in tastes. If a commodity becomes fashionable then the demand for it rises; if a commodity is successfully advertised then the demand for it will rise. There can also be a change in tastes away from a commodity (normally, though, in preference to a substitute commodity, e.g. away from Swiss balance spring watches to quartz digital watches). As we pointed out in Chapter 1, tastes can be considered as given and producers respond to them by supplying what consumers want. Other economists, such as Kenneth Galbraith in the United States, believe that large organizations can create tastes to suit what they wish to supply. If tastes are given then the demand curve does not change because of this factor; if, however, suppliers can change tastes through advertising, then demand can change because of a change in tastes.

We can conclude this section by saying that a demand curve is a relationship between the price of a commodity and the quantity demanded of that commodity. When the price rises there is a movement up the *given* demand curve, and when the price falls there is a movement down the given demand curve. In other words, a change in price leads to movements *along* a given demand curve. A demand curve will move if a number of other factors change. We shall now list all factors which lead to a shift in the demand curve to the right. (You should make a list of all factors that move the demand curve to the left.) They are:

(1) A rise in income – assuming the good is normal
(2) A rise in the price of a substitute commodity
(3) A fall in the price of a complementary commodity
(4) A change in tastes in favour of this commodity.

The market demand curve

Most of our discussion so far has been about an individual's demand curve – although we have said that a total demand curve can be obtained. Let us see exactly how. We shall consider just two households (since the same argument holds if there are one thousand or one million). Once again we present the information in the form of a table and a graph (Table 4 and Fig. 6). We distinguish the two individuals as A and B.

TABLE 4: **Market demand curve**

Price (p)	Quantity demanded by A (q^A)	Quantity demanded by B (q^B)	Total market demand ($q = q^A+q^B$)
1	55	90	145
2	50	80	130
3	45	70	115
4	40	60	100
5	35	50	85
6	30	40	70
7	25	30	55
8	20	20	40

We have labelled individual A's demand curve as D^A, and B's is labelled D^B. The total demand curve, or what we call the *market demand curve*, is labelled D. The market demand is obtained, as shown in Table 4, by adding horizontally the quantity demanded by individual A to the quantity demanded by individual B at each corresponding price. Thus, at p = \$4 we have individual A demanding 40 units and individual B demanding 60 units, giving a market demand of 100 units.

Firms are not interested in individual demands, they are concerned only about the total demand, i.e. only about market demand. This is important. A firm does not conern itself with who buys their product; they are concerned only with the fact that there are some households who wish to buy what they supply. Consequently, the market mechanism is impersonal – it does not identify individuals.

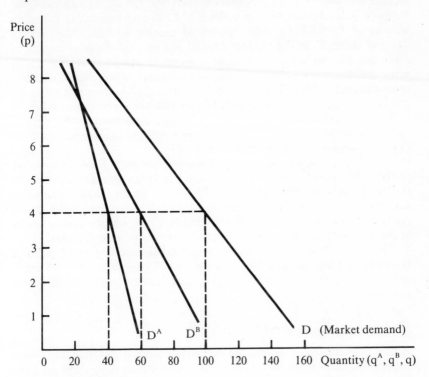

FIG. 6: **Market demand**

Even total market demand may be considered too broad. Firms have discovered that certain brands of goods sell effectively only in certain segments of the total market. Thus, a car manufacturer may segment his market into those who buy family cars and those who buy luxury cars. By segmenting the market in this way he can design and promote a product which will have the largest number of customers in each group.

We have established what factors move individual demand curves to the right (or the left). If most people in the community (or a market segment) respond in this way then the market demand curve will move in the same way. Thus, if D^A and D^B move to the right in Fig. 6, then it is clear that the market demand curve will also move to the right. Uncertainty arises only if many demand curves are shifting rightward and others leftward, but this is most unlikely.

Distribution of income

One aspect is important which arises in the market demand curve but *not* in the individual demand curves, and that is to do with the distribution of income. When we drew D^A and D^B in Fig. 6, this was for a particular level of income which each individual possessed. The total level of income was the sum of all household incomes. Let us take an example. Suppose individual A has an income of $100 and individual B has an income of $500. Then total household income is $600. The market demand curve, D in Fig. 6, does depend not only on the *total* income of $600, but also on how it is distributed. Suppose that the government, by some means, re-distributed income so individual A now has $200 while individual B has $400. Total income remains at $600. Does this mean the market demand curve is unaffected? Generally, the market demand curve *will* be affected by such a change in income distribution. We already know that if the commodity is normal then a rise in income will shift the demand curve to the right while a fall in income will shift the demand curve to the left. Since individual A's income has risen, then D^A will shift to the right. Since individual B's income has fallen then D^B will shift to the left. If, however, the rightward shift in D^A is *greater* than the leftward shift in D^B, then the market demand curve will shift to the right. If this market is for foodstuffs, we would expect that a re-distribution in favour of the poor will shift the market demand curve for food to the right.

Whether such a re-distribution should take place is part of political economy and the role attached to the state and how far it should involve itself in the market. We touched on this in Chapter 1, and we shall return to it again in Chapter 12.

Price elasticity of demand

A firm is interested in the market demand because it can determine what happens to sales when the price is raised or lowered. One thing we have established is that when the price is raised the quantity falls or when the price is lowered the quantity will rise. It would appear, then, that a producer if it wished to increase its sales would be advised to lower its price. But in lowering its price it may reduce its *total revenue*. The revenue it receives from the sales of its goods is obtained by multiplying the price by the quantity sold. This we refer to as total revenue. Table 5 sets out a number of calculations.

First we see that total revenue rises as the price rises until the price exceeds $5. Thereafter total revenue falls as the price rises. The reason for this can be seen by considering percentage changes (where here we consider only percentage increases in the price and percentage decreases in the quantity). The table shows the percentage change in price (e.g., in going from $4 to $5 we have the percentage change in price as $(5-4)/4 \times 100 = 25\%$) and the percentage change in quantity (i.e., for the same movement $(85-100)/100 \times 100 = -15\%$). We see, then, that the percentage rise in price is greater than the percentage fall in the quantity demanded and so total revenue will rise by raising the price, as shown by the fact that it rises from \$400 to \$425. This will not always be true. In raising the price from \$6 to \$7 we note that the percentage fall in the quantity demanded exceeds the percentage rise in the price. Consequently, total revenue declines from \$420 to \$385.

TABLE 5: **Price elasticity of demand***

Price (p)	Market demand (q)	Total revenue (TR=p×q)	Marginal revenue	% change in p	% change in q	Elasticity (E_d)
1	145	145	—	—	—	—
2	130	260	115	100	−10.3	0.1
3	115	345	85	50	−11.5	0.2
4	100	400	55	33.3	−13.0	0.4
5	85	425	25	25	−15.0	−0.6
6	70	420	−5	20	−17.6	−0.9
7	55	385	−35	16.7	−21.4	−1.3
8	40	320	−65	14.3	−27.3	−1.9

*Percentages are calculated for price rises (i.e., the higher price less the lower price divided by the lower price and expressed as a percentage) and quantity reductions (i.e., the lower quantity less the higher quantity divided by the lower quantity and expressed as a percentage).

We have established that if (ignoring the sign) the percentage change in the quantity demanded is less than the percentage change in the price, a rise in the price will raise revenue while a fall in the price lowers total revenue. The opposite is true when the percentage change in the quantity demanded is greater than the percentage change in the price. We can simplify this result by defining a term which is the ratio of the percentage change in the quantity demanded to the percentage change in the price. This ratio is called the *price elasticity of demand*. If we let E_d denote this ratio, then:

$$E_d = \frac{\text{percentage change in quantity demanded}}{\text{percentage change in price}}$$

Thus, if the price elasticity of demand is less than unity ($E_d < 1$) a *rise* in the price will *raise* total revenue. If, however, the price elasticity of demand is greater than unity ($E_d > 1$) then a *rise* in the price will *reduce* total revenue.

What happens when the price elasticity of demand is unity? Then the percentage change in the quantity demanded is just equal to the percentage change in the price. This means that total revenue remains constant. These different groups occur so frequently in microeconomics that we give each a name, as shown in Table 6.

By way of example, suppose the local bus company is not making sufficient revenue to cover its costs (we shall discuss costs in more detail in Chapter 4). It decides then to raise its price. Will it succeed in covering more of its costs? The answer depends on the price elasticity of demand. If demand is very price elastic, revenue will fall when the price is raised. Since this is highly probable then the bus company must be careful on its choice to raise its price.

TABLE 6: **Classification of price elasticity of demand**

Elasticity of demand*		Name
$E_d < 1$	less than unity	inelastic
$E_d > 1$	greater than unity	elastic
$E_d = 1$	unity	unit elastic

* Elasticity is defined ignoring the sign (i.e., it is always expressed as a positive number).

Tobacco, especially cigarettes, in most countries is relatively price inelastic. Given that this is true, why is such a commodity more likely to be taxed by governments in order to raise government revenue? The reason is that with a relatively inelastic demand, price can rise substantially with very little relative decline on the quantity demanded. Revenue will accordingly rise. Part, or all, of this increased revenue goes to the government in the form of tax receipts.

One aspect of the world baffles non-economists. Why in a bumper harvest do some farmers destroy some of their harvest? We can see why, in terms of our analysis so far. Many farm products have a fairly inelastic demand – arising from the fact that they are necessities. If there is a fine harvest, then supply (which we shall deal with in Chapter 5) will be plentiful. The market price will accordingly fall substantially. But if demand is price inelastic, a fall in price will reduce revenue. This can be seen in Fig. 7, where the price has fallen from p_1 to p_2 and the quantity demanded has risen from q_1 to q_2.

The revenue before the bumper harvest was $p_1 \times q_1$ and shown by the hatched area. What is important to remember is that the revenue in this case denotes the farmer's *income*. Now a good harvest which sets the price at p_2 will, in fact, *reduce* the farmer's income to $p_2 \times q_2$ (i.e. the dotted area is *less* than the hatched area). We could have predicted this simply from knowing that the demand was price inelastic. The farmer, by burning some of the crop (in fact burning $q_2 - q_3$ in Fig. 7), will gain a higher price, namely p_3, and a higher income, i.e. $p_3 \times q_3$ is *greater* than income level $p_2 \times q_2$.

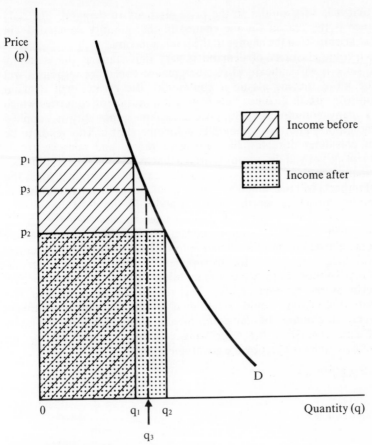

FIG. 7: **Bumper harvest**

Income elasticity of demand

One of the major determinants of the quantity demanded, other than the price, is the level of income. We have already noted that, for normal goods, as income rises then so does the quantity demanded. Now suppose income rises by 1%, what is the percentage effect on the quantity demanded? If the quantity demanded rises by less than 1% then this commodity is said to be *income inelastic*. On the other hand, if the quantity demanded rises by more than 1%, the commodity is said to be *income elastic*. If the quantity demanded also rises by 1%, we have a situation of unit income elasticity.

The income elasticity is then defined to be:

$$E_y = \frac{\text{percentage change in the quantity demanded}}{\text{percentage change in the level of income}}$$

Note that it is very similar to the price elasticity of demand. The only difference is the reason for the change in the quantity demanded – in this case arising from the change in the level of income.

The income elasticity of demand is very important as the economy grows, since it will indicate where the greatest consumer responses will be. The more income elastic a commodity the greater will demand respond to a rise in income. This is very important for countries which import many commodities. Suppose a certain commodity is supplied only by imports and this commodity is income elastic. This tends to be true of consumer durables, like transistor radios and microelectronic equipment. What will this mean? It means that as income rises so too does the demand for these imports. If imports are not constrained then the level of imports will rise, and may lead to a balance of payments problem.

Another impact is worth noting. Foodstuffs tend to be income inelastic, that is the quantity demanded rises by less than the rise in income. As income rises, therefore, consumers' demands move in favour of income elastic commodities relative to income inelastic commodities. Since this means more sales for the suppliers of income elastic commodities relative to those of inelastic commodities, a re-distribution of income will occur as the economy grows. This should not be surprising. The distribution of income would remain unaffected only in the one unlikely case where all commodities have unit income elasticities. Since we know this is not true, then for a growing economy income will be re-distributed – unless off-set by the government.

Chapter 4

The firm, production and costs

JUST AS THE INDIVIDUAL DECISION UNIT on the demand side is the household, the individual decision unit on the supply side is the *firm*. Although there may be many buyers this may not be true of the number of firms supplying a particular commodity. This means that it is possible for firms' decisions to have more far-reaching impacts. For example, if a firm decides to close down a section in area A and re-locate in area B (either in the same country or even in a different country), this can have far-reaching effects in area A. The more dependent area A is on this particular firm for employment, then the more significant its impact will be. Of course, there are favourable impacts in area B where the firm has now re-located.

It must be noted that 'the *firm*' in economic theory is a mental construct which denotes an institution which makes decisions about price and output within a market economy. It is not about a particular firm (e.g. Shell or ICI). Such a concept of the firm does not consider its internal structure. It does, however, supply some insights into the behaviour of firms. When dealing with firms in the real world, these can be owner-controlled or run by a board of directors. Where ownership is divorced from control, shares are usually issued and the firm is now often referred to as a *company*. Firms (or companies) may be sub-divided into *plants*, (smaller units which together make up the firm). In economic theory, the firm is usually assumed to produce only a single good, while most real world companies produce many goods (i.e. they are multi-product firms). In economic theory, the firm is assumed to have a decision maker, which may either be an individual or a group. How decisions are arrived at, however, is not considered. It is clear, therefore, that 'the firm' used here is a very simple construction which allows us to concentrate on just output and price decisions. This simple construction we shall retain throughout this book.

What type of decisions, then, does a firm make? These are:

(1) How best can it combine the factors of production (land, labour and capital) to produce its output?
(2) At what level of output should it produce?
(3) What price should it charge for its output?
(4) Should it advertise its product? If so, what is the most effective means of doing this?
(5) What investment should the firm undertake? How should this investment be financed?

Question (1) is about efficiency, more specifically technical efficiency. It could be re-phrased in the following manner: given the technology available at present, what is the most efficient way it can combine its factor inputs (land, labour and capital) so as to produce this output with the minimum of factor inputs? It can be put another way which is sometimes useful: given the level of technology, and given the level of the factors of production, what is the maximum output it can produce? Thus *technical efficiency* can be considered as either producing a given output with the minimum of inputs or producing the maximum output for given levels of input. However, technical efficiency is not the only consideration. Factor inputs like labour, capital and raw materials, must be purchased. To use the minimum factor inputs to produce a given output may be very costly. The microeconomist, therefore, is concerned more with *economic efficiency*. This can be taken to mean that for a given technology and a given level of output, a firm is economically efficient if it combines its factor inputs so as to produce this output at the lowest possible cost.

It may be noted that question (1) referred usually to some given level of output. But how is this level of output determined? We shall deal with this topic in this and the next chapter. A firm is concerned not only with what level of output it should produce at, but also with what price it should sell its goods for. We need to establish if it has any control over the price it sells at and what makes a firm change its price. These considerations, the building blocks of which are dealt with in this chapter, will determine the market supply curve for a commodity. Once we have built up the market supply curve we can combine it with the market demand to analyse a number of situations (see Chapter 6).

Questions (4) and (5) are beyond the scope of this book. Question (4) will be dealt with in another book in this series. Question (5), however, is a reminder that a firm, in economic theory, is an abstract idea but when applied in the real world the structure of a firm, and how the firm obtains finance, can influence the level of output chosen and the price set. It is worth pursuing this, if only briefly, as it does highlight some major changes taking place in microeconomics. These comments will also show why there are a number of theories as to the objectives pursued by firms.

A firm's objectives

The main assumption made about the goal of a firm, i.e. a firm's objective, is that *it sets out* to maximise profits. This is the equivalent assumption to households maximising their utility. If this is the *only* objective a firm has, then we do not need to consider its internal organization and how it conducts its business. Why? If the organization is too large or too small, or if it is conducting its business inefficiently, then it will not be making as much profit as it could be making. If, however, it has more than one goal, e.g. if it wishes not only to achieve adequate profits but also to grow, then its *structure, conduct and performance* matter. It is the consideration of multiple objectives which turns our attention also to the internal organization of a firm. But once we do this we enter a different realm of economics; namely, organizational theory. The point here is whether a firm, say, can achieve its many objectives by means of one type of organizational structure but not another. Does it matter, for instance, whether decisions are made at all levels in an organization or only at the top of a hierarchical system where each subsidiary decision is passed on to the next layer of the pyramid?

To what extent the stucture of an organization matters also depends on whether the firm is a private family business, whether it is a large public company issuing shares to raise financial capital or whether it is a large multinational company. Furthermore, a number of firms belong to industries which are run by the government – *nationalized industries*. In such cases the main objectives may be different from those of private firms, but also the means of finance and their structure may be determined by government bureaucracies, as we shall note in Chapter 12.

Although the microeconomist recognises these real world complications, he requires a means of bringing together relevant information about a firm's cost, production and pricing. Since profit maximisation is probably the most important objective that most firms try to achieve, although not the only one, we begin with this single objective. In this book we shall retain almost exclusively this single objective, recognizing that the results must be adapted for firms with multiple objectives. Anyone pursuing microeconomics further will see how the results must be adapted – in courses on managerial economics and/or industrial organization. However, what we deal with in the remainder of this chapter, and in Chapters 7–9, will lay the foundation for such study.

Production

Production means the technical transformation of inputs into output. Inputs are what are used in the transformation and incorporate labour, capital, raw materials and possibly outputs from other firms (e.g. steel). In broad terms inputs can be considered as part of three categories: land, labour and capital. The result of the transformation process is called output. Output can either be of a good, such as a car; or a service, such as a haircut. In the first case we refer to it as a physical commodity (or just simply a commodity). We tend, therefore, to use the terms 'goods' and 'commodities' interchangeably.

At any point in time the technical transformation of inputs into output is given. In other words, there is some known technology. This does not mean that there is only one *technique* of production. Why not? A technique of production means the various ways labour, capital and land (the factor inputs) can be combined to produce the output. Here we shall assume only one output is produced. Even so, there is a limited number of techniques. It is possible to farm land with much labour and little capital equipment or with little labour and a lot of capital equipment.

Let us illustrate the point. Suppose we wish to combine just labour and capital to produce some output, say 100 units of output. Let there be three techniques, labelled A, B and C, as shown in Table 7. Since each combination of labour and capital produces 100 units of output, then we cannot make a decision by considering the level of output. Can we make a decision if we consider inputs? We can if we take account of the input prices, i.e. the price of labour (wages) and the price of capital (the rental on capital). Additional information is now available and is contained in Table 8. This table shows that wages are $2 per unit and the price of capital is $1 per unit. Given that each technique produces 100 units of output it is clear that technique B is the one to choose. Why? Because it produces the same output as techniques A and C but at a lower *total cost* – namely, $600 as against $900 for technique A and $700 for technique C. (Notice that total cost is derived by multiplying the number of labour units by the price of labour and adding this to the number of capital units multiplied by the price of capital.)

TABLE 7: **Techniques of production**

Technique	Labour	Capital	Output
A	400	100	100
B	200	200	100
C	100	500	100

TABLE 8: **Costing techniques of production (constant output)**

Technique	Labour	Price per unit of labour	Capital	Price per unit of capital	Total cost	Average cost
A	400	2	100	1	900	9
B	200	2	200	1	600	6
C	100	2	500	1	700	7

Another way of considering this is in terms of *average cost*. Average cost is defined as the total cost divided by the number of units produced. So the average cost of each technique is:

A: $900 \div 100 = 9$ B: $600 \div 100 = 6$ C: $700 \div 100 = 7$

Again technique B gives the lowest average cost. In this example it did not matter whether we considered total or average cost. But this was only because each technique was producing the same level of output.

Now consider similar information contained in Table 9. Although technique B still has the lowest total cost, it has the highest average cost.

TABLE 9: **Costing techniques of production (differing output)**

Technique	Labour	Price per unit of labour	Capital	Price per unit of capital	Output	Average cost
A	400	2	100	1	100	9
B	200	2	200	1	50	12
C	100	2	500	1	50	14

In other words, it costs more to produce 1 unit of output using technique
B ($12) than either of A ($9) or C ($14). In this instance the firm will
produce the commodity using technique A.

We can combine both results into a single proposition:

PROPOSITION: Given technology, and given factor prices, a firm should
use that technique where average cost is lowest.

Using this proposition, then, technique B would be chosen in Table 8 and
technique A in Table 9 – which are the correct techniques to use.

A change in factor prices

What happens when the price of factor inputs changes? We can see this
by re-considering Table 8, but now suppose capital becomes relatively
more expensive (which could happen if it became scarce). Let the capital
price rise to $5 per unit. The results are now given in Table 10. We note
two results from this table. First, the average cost of all techniques has
risen. This is a general result. If one factor price rises, all else remaining
the same, then for each level of output the average cost rises. Similarly, a
fall in one factor price, all else remaining constant, will lead to a fall in
average cost for all levels of output.

The second result shown in Table 10 is that there is now a change of
technique. The smallest average cost at the higher factor price of capital
is now when technique A is used rather than technique B. The reason for
this should not be too difficult to see. In Table 10 it is to be noted that

TABLE 10: **Result on techniques of a rise in the price of capital**

Technique	Labour	Price per unit of labour	Capital	Price per unit of capital	Output	Average cost
A	400	2	100	5	100	13
B	200	2	200	5	100	14
C	100	2	500	5	100	27

technique A uses relatively less capital to labour than either of the other techniques. (We can see this explicitly by considering the capital/labour ratio. Doing this gives ratios of ¼ for A, 1 for B and 5 for C.) Consequently, when the price of capital rises the technique to favour is the one using relatively less capital since this is now relatively more expensive. This is seen very strongly in the substantial rise in the average cost of technique C, which arises because this technique is very capital intensive relative to the other two techniques.

These two results are very important and you should ensure you understand them clearly. To ensure this, establish that if the information in Table 9 is true, but that the price of labour rises to $5 per unit, then average cost rises for all levels of output and that technique C becomes the least-cost technique. Make sure you understand why there is a move to technique C by considering the labour/capital ratio for each technique.

Total costs, average costs and marginal costs

So far we have concentrated on production and the choice of technique, given the technology and given the factor input prices. It is clear, however, that costs in general will vary with the level of output produced. The greater the level of output the higher the total cost of producing that level of output. There are three important costs which are related to the level of output: total costs, average costs and marginal costs.

In fact all the information can be obtained from total costs. As we have already noted, total costs are obtained by multiplying all the factor inputs by their respective prices. It is, however, more convenient to consider costs in terms of *fixed costs* and *variable costs*, i.e. costs which are fixed regardless of the level of output and costs that vary directly with the level of output. In the first category one usually thinks of the rent for land and buildings, insurance against fire and theft, etc. These are the same whether the firm produces nothing or is working at full capacity. Variable costs are attached to the factor inputs which vary as output varies. For instance, more output usually requires more labour and/or more capital, and so these would be part of variable costs. The greater the output, the more a firm will require of at least one input. As we shall see, variable costs are important in establishing marginal costs.

We can distinguish these various costs with the help of Table 11. First let us establish how average and marginal costs are derived in the table. Average cost is the total cost divided by the number of units produced. Thus, the total cost of producing 4 units is $88 and so the average cost per unit at the output level of 4 units is:

$$\frac{\text{total cost}}{\text{output}} = \frac{88}{4} = 22$$

Notice that the average cost per unit declines initially as output rises, and then rises after 5 units of output.

TABLE 11: **Total, average and marginal costs**

Output	Total cost	Average cost	Marginal cost
1	52	52	—
2	76	38	24
3	84	28	8
4	88	22	4
5	100	20	12
6	132	22	32
7	196	28	64
8	304	38	108
9	468	52	164

Marginal cost is less straightforward. This is the additional cost of producing one more unit. Thus, in going from output level 1 to output level 2, costs rose by an additional $24. Thus the second unit of output put an extra $24 onto total costs. This we call marginal cost. Similarly

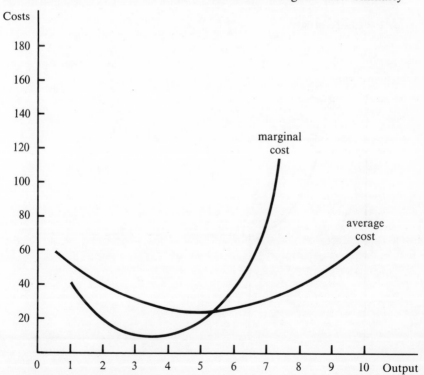

FIG. 8: **Average and marginal cost**

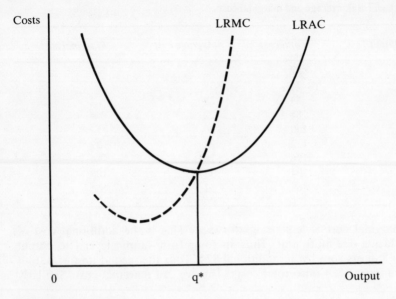

(a) U-shaped cost curves

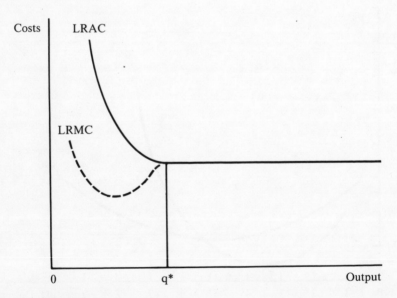

(b) L-shaped cost curves

FIG. 9: **U-shaped and L-shaped cost curves**

the third unit added an extra $8 to total cost and so the marginal cost of the third unit is $8. It will be noted that the marginal cost also declines initially and then begins to rise.

It will be useful not only in constructing a supply curve but also in analysing price and output decisions, which we shall do in Chapters 7–9, to draw average and marginal costs. This we do in Fig. 8 (see page 37), where we have plotted the results of Table 11 – but we have joined up all the observations with continuous curves (also notice that we have marked the marginal costs half-way between each output level). These are fairly standard shapes for average and marginal cost curves.

Why does the average cost curve initially fall? The reason lies in the fact that fixed costs are being spread over a greater output level; in addition variable costs are rising by less for these early units of output because factor inputs can be combined more efficiently. These together mean average costs are falling. But why should average costs rise for larger levels of output? This is more debatable. The reason usually given is that as a firm grows it becomes more difficult for management to choose how best to combine factor inputs and the decision-making of the firm becomes more complex. Some argue that this does not occur and average cost simply reaches a minimum and then levels off, forming an L-shaped average cost curve (see Fig. 9(b)).

There will be some output level at which average costs are at a minimum. At this level output is at its optimum – in the sense that if less were produced then average cost would be higher and if more were produced then average cost would be higher. If the average cost curve is L-shaped then there is no single minimum. In this case we refer to the *minimum efficient scale of output*, which is that output level where the average cost first reaches its lowest point.

To summarise: average and marginal costs change with output. Generally, both curves are U-shaped but may in practice be L-shaped. Marginal cost cuts the average cost at its minimum point. The lowest point on the average cost curve is the optimal level of output (or the minimum efficient scale at the output level at which average cost is first minimised).

Short run and long run costs

We have not so far distinguished over what time period the costs refer to. It is very important, however, to do so. Two time periods are distinguished: the short run and the long run. These are not time periods in the sense of days, weeks or months, but are based on whether some factor inputs are fixed or variable. If at least one factor input is fixed then we are referring to the short run. If all factor inputs are variable then we are dealing with the long run. Thus, the distinguishing feature is whether a factor input is fixed (the short run) or all are variable (the long run).

The distinction is best considered in terms of a firm with fixed capital (and management) but which can vary the labour it employs. The fact that capital is fixed means we are dealing with the short run because, clearly, it is possible to vary this in a longer period. This does mean that in the short run capital also becomes part of fixed costs and the only variable cost is the payment in wages.

Let us consider the short run in more detail. Suppose the only variable factor is labour – with capital and other factor inputs held fixed. Now let labour be raised by one unit. This will lead to some additional output. The additional output arising from the additional unit of labour employed is referred to as the *marginal physical product of labour*. Let this be from adding 1 unit of labour to 100 units. Now add another unit of labour (the 102nd unit). This further additional person will also lead to extra output. But will the additional output of the 102nd person, the marginal physical product of labour of the 102nd person, be smaller, larger or the same as the 101st person? In general we would expect for early units of labour that the marginal physical product of labour would increase because more efficient methods can be implemented and greater division of labour can be practised.

'Division of labour' means that, instead of one person, or a few, doing all the work involved in producing a good the work is split into separate jobs, and each person does one job only. Work is passed from one person to another. Each worker soon becomes highly skilled in his job. More machinery can be used, so speeding up production. Car assembly lines are, perhaps, the ultimate in division of labour. There comes a point, however, when the extra labour simply becomes a nuisance (they get in each others' way or more disputes break out). Although more in total is produced, at this stage each extra person contributes less and less to total output. In other words, the marginal physical product of labour declines. This is a general result attached to varying a factor input with other factors held constant. Thus, if capital is increased by one unit with labour held fixed then we have extra output – called the *marginal physical product of capital*.

Here too, there will come a point where the marginal physical product of capital declines. A decline in the marginal physical product of a fixed factor is one reason why the short-run marginal cost curve rises after a certain level of output. Since the marginal physical product of labour, say, is declining then each extra unit of output requires yet additional labour to produce it and although all units of labour are paid at a constant wage, this extra labour means that marginal cost is rising. An example may help to see this.

Suppose the 101st unit of labour produces 1 unit of output while the 102nd unit of labour produces 0.5 units of output, the 103rd 0.3 units and the 104th 0.2 units of output. Let labour be paid at $2 per person. Then the marginal cost of producing one extra unit of output is $2 since this 1 unit can be produced in going from 100 to 101 units of labour input. But what about a second extra unit of output? This next unit of output requires a second, third and fourth unit of labour (giving marginal products of 0.5, 0.3 and 0.2 – a total of 1 unit of output). Thus, the marginal cost of this second extra unit of output is 3 units of labour multiplied by $2, giving a total of $6. We see, then, that a declining marginal physical product of a factor leads to a rise in the marginal cost of producing extra output. Note that a rise in the marginal physical product of a factor, which occurred in the early ranges of employing this factor, leads to a fall in the short-run marginal cost.

This explains why the short-run marginal cost curve takes on a U-shape. It also explains why the short-run average cost eventually rises. Although in the initial ranges of output the fixed costs are spread over a greater level of output, the rising marginal cost of producing extra output pushes up the average cost. Eventually, this rising marginal cost swamps any fall from declining average fixed costs (i.e. total fixed costs divided by output) so raising over-all average costs.

To summarise, the short run is distinguished by having at least one factor input constant. When a variable factor is raised with other factors held constant, the extra output from this variable factor (the marginal physical product of this variable factor) first rises but eventually declines. The rise and then fall of the marginal physical product of a variable factor, other factors held constant, explains why the short-run average cost curve is U-shaped and why the short-run marginal cost curve is also U-shaped. Both of these shapes are shown in Fig. 8 (page 37), where we now explicitly refer to the curves as short run.

The long run is characterized by the fact that all factors of production are variable. This means that we can vary capital as well as labour, build more plants, and increase the size of management. This brings us to a very important topic: namely, *economies of scale*. By scale we mean increasing *all* factor inputs in the same proportion, e.g. doubling all factor inputs.

To see this point, first consider a box with sides of 1cm each. The surface area is $6 \times 1 = 6 \text{cm}^2$ (since a box, including the lid, has six sides each of $1 \times 1 = 1 \text{cm}^2$ in area). The volume, however, is 1cm^3 (i.e. $1 \times 1 \times 1 = 1 \text{cm}^3$). Now double the size of the box to 2cm. The surface area increases to $6 \times 2 = 12 \text{cm}^2$ while the volume increase to $2 \times 2 \times 2 = 8 \text{cm}^3$. Thus, the surface area doubles but the volume increases eight fold. If we consider an oil tanker or a ship carrying grain, we see that the carrying capacity increases substantially for a small increase in the ship's size. This will lower the average cost of carrying oil or grain.

Similarly, a firm can double in size. Its output, however, can more than double, just double, or increase by less than double. For a doubling of factor inputs the three possible changes in output each have a name:

Change in output	Name
less than twice	decreasing returns to scale
just twice	constant returns to scale
more than twice	increasing returns to scale

The more important one is where output more than doubles when all factor inputs are doubled. How can such increasing returns to scale come about? The most usual explanations are more efficient techniques and division of labour. It may be that only with a large plant is it worth while using large machines. Although these can produce more, only if your sales warrant this will it be worth while purchasing one. (An everyday example may help. You may find a typewriter suitable for your essays. A microcomputer can now do the same job and better. But would you invest in one? You might only if you did a great deal of writing to warrant the cost of a microcomputer.) Only when a firm is of a certain size can machines and labour be specialised. If labour is specialised then it can become more effective. Similarly, if a machine is specialised then production does not have to stop as it is switched from one type of job to another.

These economies of scale will reduce the average cost as the size of output expands. There may come a point, however, where specialisation leads to psychological problems for labour, possibly as the result of boredom, where management becomes too bureaucratic and where machines become so specialised that few people can work them. All these may, after a certain level of output, lead to diseconomies of scale. In other words, average cost begins to rise. If this occurs then the long-run average cost curve is U-shaped. It may, as we mentioned earlier, level out and be L-shaped. This, however, is true only of the long-run average cost curve.

One final point is worth making. In Fig. 8 we marked the optimal level of output. This refers *only* to the long run. Microeconomists talk of the *minimum efficient scale* of plant or firm. This is where long-run average cost is at a minimum or where the long-run average cost first levels off, as shown in Fig. 9(b) by q* (see page 38). This concept is very important in considering how many firms an industry can sustain at such efficient levels. Suppose, for instance, that we knew the market demand for some commodity was 100 units. Suppose further that the minimum efficient scale was 50 units. Then just two firms each of minimum efficient scale could supply the market demand. If we observed, say, five firms in the industry then it would be almost certain that at most one and probably none were at their minimum efficient scale. We would know immediately that they would not be at their minimum long-run average cost.

Since in the long run all factor inputs can be varied then it is always possible to produce a given output in the long run at least as cheaply as in the short run. Even when short-run average costs are at a minimum, it is still possible to produce this output at a lower average cost – except for the firm which is, in the short run, at its optimal size ($SRAC_2$ in Fig. 10). In Fig. 10 we show the short-run and long-run situations. In this figure we have three short-run average cost curves, denoted SRAC, and the long-run average cost curve, denoted LRAC. Output level q_1 can be produced in the short run at minimum cost C_s while in the long run the

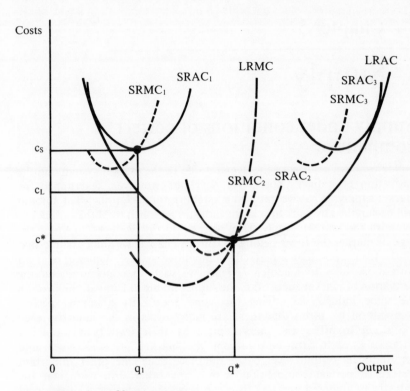

FIG. 10: Short run and long run costs

same output can be produced at cost C_L. But even this long run cost can be improved on if the scale of the plant is raised to q* giving a long run *and* short run average cost of C*.

To summarise, long run average costs fall as economies of scale are reaped but may rise as diseconomies of scale set in. The optimal plant size is given where long run average cost is at a minimum and this is important for assessing how many such optimum-sized firms can be sustained by a given market. The cost of producing *any* level of output (except the optimum level) is lower in the long run than in the short run. This is because in the long run all factors can be varied and more efficient means of production can be found. The long-run average cost is constructed for a given technology and for a given set of factor prices. A rise in factor prices raises both the short-run and the long-run average cost curves; it also raises the short-run and long-run marginal cost curves.

Chapter 5

Supply

Supply under conditions of perfect competition

So far we have dealt with the demand side of the market system and the derivation of a firm's costs. We have not, however, determined the market supply. What we must do is establish for each price what amount will be supplied by each firm in the industry and then total the supplies to establish the market supply. However, to do this we need to know the type of market the firms belong to. In this chapter we shall assume that all the firms operate in a perfectly competitive market. This will be dealt with more fully in Chapter 7. Here we wish to concentrate on the derivation of market supply (i.e. the supply obtained from all the firms in the same industry supplying the same good). By assuming perfect competition we mean that there are' many firms in the industry, each too small to affect the market price by their own behaviour. Put differently, each firm must accept the market price as given and determine its output level based on this price. One other important feature of perfect competition is that any other firm can enter the industry unhindered and any firm can leave the industry: a situation of perfect entry and exit. Finally, it is assumed that firms operate in such a manner as to maximize profits.

The implication of these assumptions is shown in Fig. 11 (see page 45), where we have the short run average cost curve (SRAC) and the short run marginal cost curve (SRMC).

Now suppose the price were $46, what would the firm supply? First we note that this price is fixed for the firm and so no matter what it sells each unit will bring into the firm $46. Suppose it supplies just 5 units. The additional cost to the firm of the fifth unit is just $20, i.e. the marginal cost of the fifth unit is $20. This means that the fifth unit will bring in to the firm $46 in revenue but will cost only an additional $20 to produce. If, on the other hand, it sold 7 units then the seventh unit would also bring into the firm $46 but it would cost an additional $84. The fifth unit, then, still gives a profit while the seventh unit leads to a loss. What about the sixth unit? The sixth unit costs an additional $46 and this is what the firm receives in payment for the sixth unit sold. Consequently, if the firm wishes to maximize its profits it will, under perfect competition, produce up to the point where the price is equal to the marginal cost. If marginal cost is less than the price then additional profits can be made by raising output; if marginal cost is greater than price then additional profits can

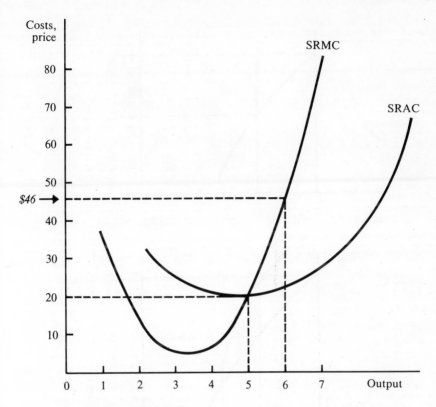

FIG. 11: **Determining a firm's supply**

be made by reducing output. (Notice with the seventh unit that this leads to a loss on that unit but total profits are still positive. We shall deal with this more fully in Chapter 7.)

The conclusion we draw is that if price is $46 then the firm will supply 6 units. If the price is $20 then by the same reasoning the firm will supply 5 units. The supply curve for the firm, then, is the marginal cost curve. It must be emphasized that this is only under the market structure called 'perfect competition'.

Now since each firm faces the same price we can establish the quantity supplied by each firm and add these together to establish the market supply. Such a market supply curve is shown in Fig. 12(c) (see page 46). This is derived as follows. There are just two representative firms, which we have called firm A and firm B. Take the price $10. At this price firm A will supply 10 units of output and firm B will supply 15 units of output. The total market supply, therefore, at the price of $10 is 25. Now consider a higher price of $15. At this price firm A is willing to supply 20 units while firm B is willing to supply 25 units. At the price of $15 the total market supply is, therefore, 45 units. If we do this for each price we

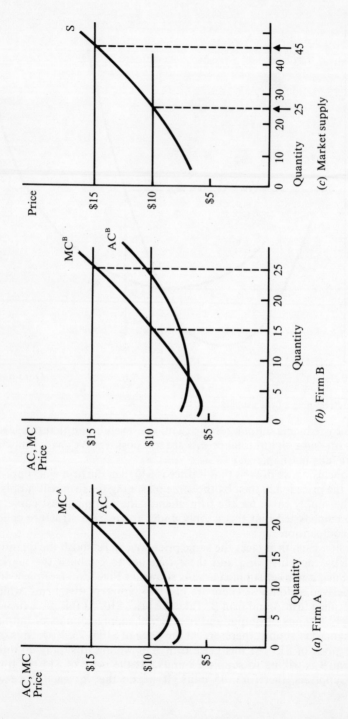

FIG. 12: **Market supply curve**

construct the market supply curve, denoted S in Fig. 12(c). Notice that this is upward sloping. The greater the price the more the market will supply. Also notice that, like demand, it is a relationship between price and quantity supplied. The quantity supplied is a flow in the sense that it represents supply per period of time (such as a year).

The market supply curve can be interpreted in another way. A given quantity, say 25 units, can be supplied at the minimum price of $10. Why is this? Clearly firm A would be happy to receive a payment in excess of $10 for the tenth unit and firm B would be happy to receive a payment in excess of $10 for the fifteenth unit, since in both cases profits would be higher. Therefore, the market would be willing to supply 25 units for a price in excess of $10. But given the industry's costs, the market will not supply 25 units for less than $10 each.

Elasticity of supply

How responsive is the market supply to a change in price? In other words, if the price changes will the industry change its supply by a small amount or by a large amount? What we require is a measure of such responsiveness. The measure used is the *elasticity of supply*. Defined:

$$E_s = \frac{\text{percentage change in quantity supplied}}{\text{percentage change in price}}$$

Suppose, for example that the price rises from $150 to $160 and the quantity supplied rises from 10 to 12. Then

$$E_s = \frac{(12-10)\times100 \div (160-150)\times100}{10 \qquad\qquad 150}$$
$$= 20 \div 6\tfrac{2}{3} = 3$$

Three categories are of particular note:*

$$0 < E_s < 1 \qquad \text{inelastic supply}$$
$$E_s = 1 \qquad \text{unit elastic}$$
$$E_s > 1 \qquad \text{elastic supply}$$

In the inelastic case the percentage change in the quantity supplied is less than the percentage change in the price. A unit elastic supply, which denotes an equal percentage change in both quantity supplied and price, divides the other two categories. An elastic supply means that the percentage change in the quantity supplied is very responsive to a change in the price.

How important are these measures? Consider a catch of fish. No matter what this year's price happened to be the supply of fish would be the same. In this extreme case the supply curve is vertical and the elasticity measure is zero. This is because the percentage change in the

* The notation < means 'is less than', and > means 'is greater than'.

quantity supplied is zero regardless of the percentage change in the price. The opposite situation is where the price remains fixed and the supply curve is horizontal. This is an *infinite elasticity of supply* because, regardless of the percentage change in the quantity supplied, the price change always remains zero (since the price is constant). The situation of a totally elastic supply is typical of the situation of grain and commodities sold on world markets. The supply to the *home market* is infinitely elastic in the sense that for a small country it cannot influence the price at which the commodity is supplied (the price being determined by the demand for and supply of the good at the world level); and so from the domestic point of view the supply is infinite at the world price. This is indicated by $E_s = \infty$ in Fig. 13.

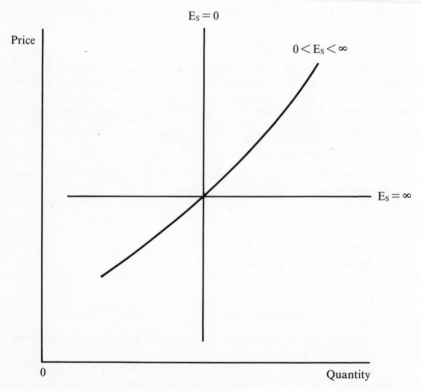

FIG. 13: **Supply curves of different elasticities**

In general we would expect agricultural commodities supplied on the home market to be less responsive to price changes than manufactured commodities. However, the more specialized the capital equipment the less responsive supply will be of manufactured commodities. This also arises because in the short run at least one factor input is fixed. If we assume this is capital, such as machines, then even if the price rises firms are limited in how much they can increase supply. They can hire more labour until the machines are fully utilized, and may engage in overtime, but these are purely short run solutions.

Long run and short run elasticities of supply

From what has just been said it is clear that it is possible to raise the level of supply in the long run by changing the level of the fixed factor. For a rise in price it is possible for firms to take on more machines and expand production and it is also possible for new firms to enter the industry. For a fall in price it is possible, in the long run, for capital and other factors of production to be laid off and also for some firms to leave the industry. Thus, the long run supply will be more elastic than the short run supply. This is shown in Fig. 14 which indicates that for a rise in price from $150 to $160 (a rise of 6⅔%) the percentage change in the quantity supplied in the short run is 20% (i.e. $(12-10) \times 100 \div 10$) while in the long run it is 50%

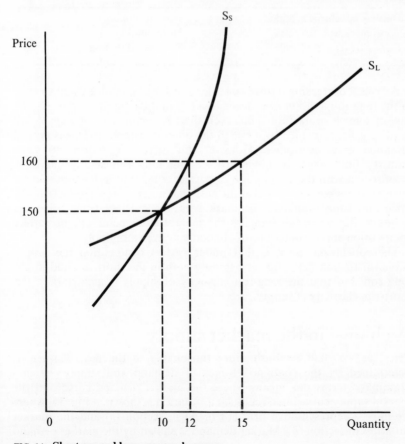

FIG. 14: **Short run and long run supply curves**

(i.e. (15–10)×100÷10). The short run supply elasticity is 3 while the long run supply elasticity is 7½.

Although the short run supply curve is upward sloping, being derived from marginal cost curves, what about the long run supply curve? Must this also be upward sloping? This depends on the economies of scale we discussed in Chapter 4. Since in the long run all costs must be covered then what matters in establishing the long run supply is not marginal cost but rather average cost. We noted in Chapter 4 that average costs in the long run can fall, rise or remain constant depending on whether the industry exhibits increasing returns to scale, decreasing returns to scale or constant returns to scale. These scale conditions and the general shape of the long run supply curve are shown in Table 12.

TABLE 12: **Scale economies and the shape of the long run supply curve**

Scale economies	Shape of long run supply curve
Decreasing returns to scale	Upward sloping
Constant returns to scale	Horizontal
Increasing returns to scale	Downward sloping

A typical decreasing returns to scale industry is agriculture and so even in the long run a fall in price leads to a fall in the long run supply. In the case of some manufacturers, however, there are economies of scale. A fall in price is accompanied by a rise in the quantity supplied. This is typical of some microelectronics. However, an increasing returns to scale industry (and hence a downward sloping long run supply curve) is inconsistent with the assumption of perfect competition. If economies of scale are possible then it is also the case that a firm can keep lowering its price and soon dominate the market as less efficient firms leave the industry. But when this happens the market stops being one of perfect competition and becomes one of oligopoly or even monopoly.

The conclusion, then, is that under perfect competition the supply curve for the market is upward sloping both in the short run and in the long run, but that the long-run elasticity of supply is greater than the short-run elasticity of supply.

A change in the market supply

Price, as we shall establish more thoroughly in the next chapter, is determined by the combined forces of demand and supply. In diagrammatic terms this means where the market demand curve and the market supply curve intersect. Such a situation is shown in Fig. 15, where we have a representative firm (Firm A) in section (*a*) and the market situation in section (*b*). Market demand is shown by the market demand

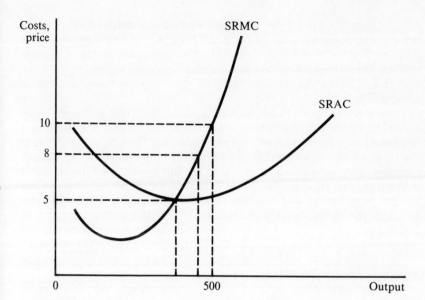

(a) Firm A

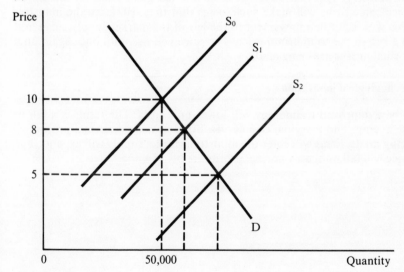

(b) Industry

FIG. 15: **Change in market supply**

curve D while the initial market supply is given by S_0. At this equilibrium the market price is \$10 and the market demand and supply is 50,000 units. At \$10 Firm A must accept this price as given and determines its level of output accordingly. The profit maximizing output level is where price equals marginal cost. At price $10 Firm A will maximize its profits if it supplies 500 units. But at this price the firm is earning supranormal profits. This is because the average revenue it receives is equal to the price and this is above the average cost (we shall expand this statement in Chapter 7).

Since there are firms like Firm A making supranormal profits then this will attract firms into the industry. This additional supply will result in a rightward shift in the industry supply curve, say from S_o to S_1. What is the result of this new entry? It is a reduction in the market price. In our example the price will fall from $10 to $8. But even at $8 Firm A is still making supranormal profits. More firms will enter the industry and the market supply curve will continue to move to the right. When will there be no further firms entering the industry? Once the market supply is S_2 and the price is $5 Firm A is no longer making supranormal profits. At this point there will be no incentive for further firms to enter the industry.

A change in factor price and market supply

Given a situation of equilibrium, suppose wage costs rise in all firms in the industry. This raises average costs and marginal costs. At the intitial price some firms will make such losses that they will leave the industry. This will result in a movement to the left of the market supply curve and to a rise in the equilibrium price. The price will rise until once again only normal profits are being made.

Technological innovation

A new improved technology will lower unit costs. The result is a fall in the average and marginal cost curves. Since now supranormal profits are being made, firms will enter the industry. Market supply will expand. The price will fall until only normal profits are being made.

Chapter 6

Demand and supply

WE HAVE ESTABLISHED both a market demand curve and a market supply curve. Why is the price determined by the intersection of these two curves? This we shall show in the first section. By means of this analysis we can answer such questions as:

(1) What is the effect of a tax or a subsidy?
(2) What is the effect of an increase/decrease in demand?
(3) What is the level of imports?

The market price

The demand curve represents the maximum price that consumers are willing to pay for a particular quantity; the supply curve is the minimum price producers are willing to accept for a given quantity. Consider the situation in Fig. 16 (see page 54). At price $6 suppliers are willing to supply on to the market 12 units while consumers wish to demand only 8 units. These are only *intended purchases*: they are what producers would like to supply and what consumers would like to consume. We assume that because there is excess supply the price will be bid down: consumers asking for a lower price and/or suppliers lowering the asking price. Similarly, we assume that if there is excess demand suppliers will raise their asking price while demanders will be prepared to pay a higher price in order to acquire the limited supply. We see, therefore, that when there is excess supply the price will fall; while when there is excess demand the price will rise. Only when there is no excess demand or supply will the price remain constant. This is where demand equals supply and the price where this occurs is called the *equilibrium price* or *market price*. Notice that at the equilibrium price the quantity demanded by consumers just matches the quantity supplied and this equilibrium quantity is the market quantity bought and sold. In Fig. 16 the equilibrium price is $5 and the equilibrium quantity is 10 units.

Before leaving this discussion, what happens if the price is artificially set at a disequilibrium rate? Suppose, for instance, a minimum price of $6 was set by the government. We see that at this price there is an excess supply. Suppliers are willing to supply 12 units but consumers wish to purchase only 8 units. The excess supply (4 units) will either perish, if it is some form of foodstuff, or be stock-piled, if it is not perishable. On the other hand, it is possible that this excess supply could be exported.

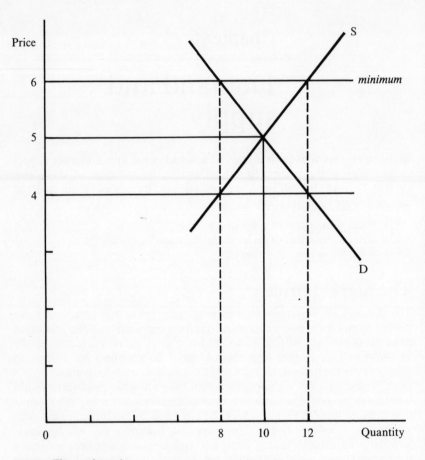

FIG. 16: **The market price**

The effect of a tax and a subsidy

Suppose the government imposes a tax on every unit sold. What is the result of this? Will the price rise by the full amount of the tax? We can answer such questions by means of demand and supply. In Fig. 17 the situation without the tax is given by demand curve D and Supply S_0. If left to itself the market would settle down at an equilibrium price of $5 and quantity bought and sold of 10 units.

For purposes of illustration consider 6 units being supplied. At this quantity the minimum price at which suppliers are willing to supply is $3. If the government imposes a tax of $2 on each unit sold then 6 units will be supplied at $5. Similarly, 10 units will be supplied at $7 ($5 plus a tax of $2). Thus the supply curve S_1 is above S_0 by the amount of the tax, namely $2.

Having established that the supply curve inclusive of the tax is S_1, we can now determine the new price and quantity. This is where S_1 intersects D. The price will rise to $6 and the quantity will fall to 8 units. The first thing we notice about the price rise is that it is less than the tax. In our illustration the price rose from $5 to $6, a rise of $1, while the tax was in fact $2. Why is this? In the situation where the price is $5 but the supply curve is S_1 the intended supply is 6 units while intended demand is 10 units. There is, therefore, an excess demand. The price will be bid up. It will be bid up until demand equals supply, which occurs at $6. The extent to which the price is bid up depends on the elasticity of demand.

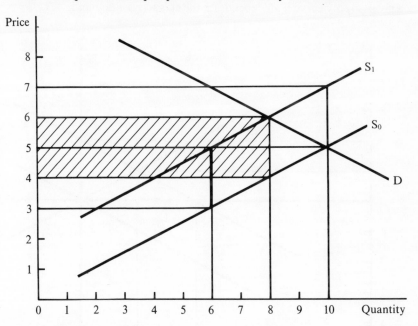

FIG. 17: **Effect of a tax/subsidy**

To see this consider the situation in Fig. 18 (see page 56). We have three different possible demand curves: D_1, D_2 and D_3. D_1 is the situation shown in Fig. 17. D_2 is a situation of an infinitely elastic demand. In this instance competition for the available supply is so great the price cannot diverge from $5. In this case the price is demand-determined and *all* the tax must be borne by the producers. The result is a fall in supply from 10 units to 6 units. Where demand is D_3 then demand is totally inelastic. No matter what the price, consumers wish to purchase only 10 units. In this case the price is supply determined and the price rises to $7, and consumers bear all the tax.

We see, then, that for the more usual situation of a downward sloping demand curve the price does not rise by the full amount of the tax and demanders and suppliers share the tax. In Fig. 17 they share the tax equally. To see this consider the equilibrium quantity and price. The equilibrium quantity is 8 units. This quantity would normally be supplied at a price of $4 but is in fact sold at $6. The total tax paid is therefore $2×8=$16. However, consumers would have paid $5 for their 8 units and so they are paying in tax a total of $1×8=$8. Suppliers on the other hand would formerly have sold these units for $5 but can now sell them for only $4, so they lose $1×8=$8. The extra paid by consumers ($8) and the loss by producers ($8) equals the total tax paid. Of course, the burden need not be shared equally as in Fig. 17. As Fig. 18 indicates, for a given supply curve it all depends on the elasticity of demand.

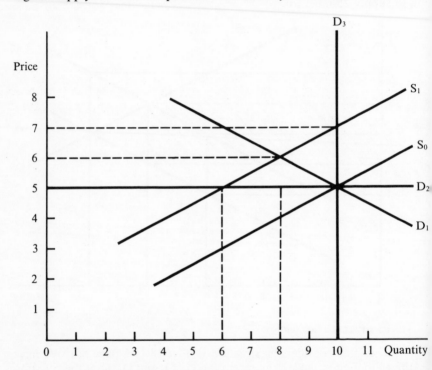

FIG. 18: A tax and different elasticities of demand

The subsidy is the mirror image of the tax. We shall be brief and use Fig. 17 again. This time let S_1 denote the initial situation. We begin with equilibrium price $6 and equilibrium quantity of 8 units. Consider 6 units. Producers are willing to supply on to the market 6 units at a minimum price of $5. If a subsidy of $2 is paid on each unit then the producer can sell 6 units for $3 knowing that it will receive an extra $2 in subsidy. Similarly, 8 units can be sold for $4 instead of $6. Thus, S_0 is the supply curve inclusive of the subsidy. The result is a rise in the quantity supplied and a fall in the equilibrium price. Notice, however, that although the two situations appear mirror images, the total tax received and the total subsidy payment are not equal. In the present situation of the subsidy, 10 units are sold. The supplier is selling them at $5 but receives $2 in subsidy on each unit sold. The total subsidy payment is, therefore, $2×10=$20.

A subsidy on each unit sold is more effective in raising consumption the more elastic the demand curve. If demand is fairly inelastic, then a per unit subsidy will not raise equilibrium sales very much. The result will be a marginal increase in the consumption of such a staple commodity and producers will receive the bulk of the subsidy.

A change in demand

Consider the situation in Fig. 19. The initial situation is with demand curve D_0 and supply S. An increase in demand raises the equilibrium price to $6 and the equilibrium quantity to 12 units.

This might occur if there is a rise in income. So long as the good is normal, a rise in income will raise consumption and so lead to an increase

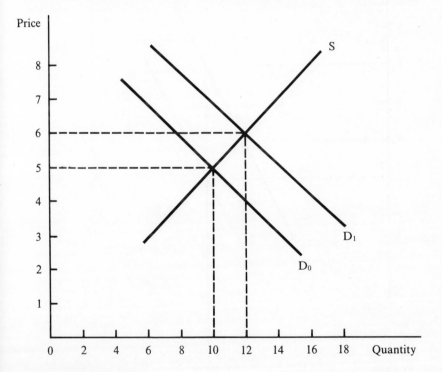

FIG. 19: **Change in demand**

in demand. It could also arise if the price of a substitute good rises. If fish becomes more expensive and people accordingly consume more meat, then there will be an increase in the demand for meat.

The effect on price and quantity of a rise in demand depends on the elasticity of supply. A totally inelastic supply (a vertical supply curve) will result in a sharp rise in the price and no change in the quantity bought and sold. In the case of a totally elastic supply curve there will be no change in the price and a sharp rise in the quantity bought and sold. (You should draw these situations yourself to verify the statements.)

Result of a bad/good harvest

The present analysis is very useful for analyzing typical agricultural situations. In Fig. 20 the initial situation is given by D and S_0. Now suppose there is a bad harvest so that in the following year supply is given by S_1. The price rises from \$5 to \$6 and the quantity bought and sold falls to 8 units.

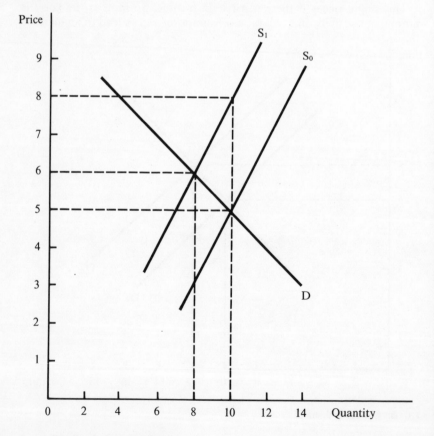

FIG. 20: **Result of a bad/good harvest**

What about the income to farmers? Farmers' income is the revenue received. In our present example, the initial revenue is $5×10=$50 and in the following year, after the bad harvest, it is $6×8=$48. It would appear, then, that not only do consumers have to pay more when there is a bad harvest but that farmers' income falls too. But the result for farmers' income may or may not be a fall.

To see why this is so, let us take an extreme case where demand is infinitely inelastic, then the bad harvest would push the price up to $8 and purchases would remain at 10 units. The farmers' revenue would then be $8×10=$80 – a rise of $30 over the 'good' year.

Can we establish some means of determining when the income of farmers will rise or fall? First, let us work out the elasticity of demand in the example in Fig. 20. It is:

$$E_d = \frac{\% \text{ change in quantity demanded}}{\% \text{ change in price}} = \frac{[(10-8)\times100]\div8}{[(6-5)\times100]\div5} = 1\frac{1}{4}$$

In this case we have an elastic demand ($E_d>1$) and a bad harvest led to a fall in income received by farmers. We also know that for a totally inelastic demand that the farmers' incomes rise for a bad harvest. In general, therefore, farmers' incomes will, for a bad harvest, fall when demand is elastic and rise when it is inelastic. When demand is unit elastic then farmers' revenues will remain unchanged.

The opposite situation occurs for a good harvest. In this case supply rises, the equilibrium price falls and purchases increase. A good harvest, then, seems good for consumers. But what about farmers' incomes? If demand is elastic then farmers' incomes will rise, but if demand is inelastic then farmers' incomes will fall when the harvest is good. Since many food-stuffs are relatively price inelastic the likely result of a good harvest is a fall in farmers' incomes. It is for this reason that one sometimes observes some farmers attempting to limit supply when the harvest is good – even to the extent of burning some of the crop! This apparent irrational behaviour is straightforward to understand in the present context, even though the moral implications may not be approved of.

Imports

Let us consider one final example to see how we can apply demand and supply analysis. In Fig. 21 (see page 60) demand D^H represents the home demand and S^H represents the home supply of some commodity. If the economy did not trade, then the price would settle, say, at $10 and the quantity bought and sold at 10 units. Now suppose the country is a small country and can import this commodity at the world price, $p^w=$5. (This means that the terms of trade do not change as a result of the trade taking place, and so all units are bought and sold at the one price of $5.) Because

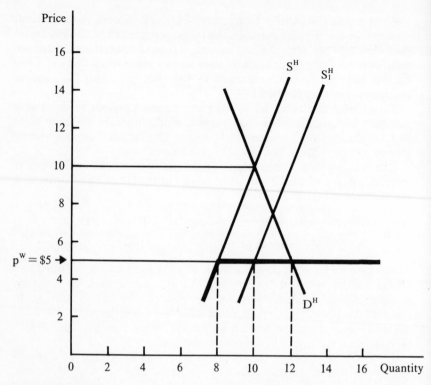

FIG. 21: **Imports**

it is the world price that is given, the supply curve becomes infinitely elastic at $5.

At the world price of $5, home demand is 12 units and home supply is 8 units. The additional 4 units are supplied by the world market in the form of imports.

We immediately see that the price consumers pay is lower when imports are allowed ($5 rather than $10). However, home supply is less (8 units rather than 10 units). The income received by home suppliers is smaller ($5×8=$40 rather than $10×10=$100) and so too may be employment. Furthermore, if such imports are not matched by exports then there may also be a deficit on the balance of payments. If, however, they are matched by exports then no such problem on the balance of payments may arise.

If a government feels for some reason that imports are too large, one policy commonly applied is to subsidize home producers. We already know that a subsidy lowers the supply curve. Let this be denoted S_1^H in Fig. 21, a subsidy of $5 per unit. The world price still remains at $5 but now home production is 10 units and imports are 2 units. Of course, the government must find the subsidy payment of $5×10=$50.

Chapter 7

Perfect competition

WE HAVE REPEATEDLY MADE THE POINT that a firm is just one element in an industry and that what matters when discussing price and output decisions is the type of market structure the firm belongs to. Market structure can be defined in terms of a variety of characteristics, such as the number of firms. Where there is a very large number we think of *perfect competition* (although the number alone is not sufficient to identify a specific type of structure); *duopoly* as two suppliers and *monopoly* as one supplier. *Oligopoly* can be considered as being a few firms. However, what characterizes the different market structures most clearly is the interrelated behaviour assumed. In perfect competition the firm has no effect on the decision-making of any other firm. For this to be the case the number of firms must be large and there must be perfect entry and exit of firms into and out of the industry.

In the case of the monopolist, covered more fully in the next chapter, he has to consider only his own behaviour in relation to what consumers will accept. In a situation of oligopoly the most characteristic feature is that a firm must take into account how its decisions will influence other firms' behaviour in the same industry and in turn how it will respond to their behaviour. There is no single form of oligopoly because there is such a variety of feasible assumptions about the form of interdependence between such firms. We shall deal with oligopoly in Chapter 9.

We can think, then, of market structure with monopoly at one end of the range and perfect competition at the other: from one firm to many firms, the range in between comprising oligopoly (including duopoly) where the number of firms is small enough to allow each to influence the behaviour of another. Sometimes the range beyond perfect competition is called imperfect competition (and it includes monopoly).

In this chapter we shall concentrate on perfect competition. Before this, however, let us investigate average, marginal and total revenue which is important for all discussions of market structure dealt with in this and the next two chapters.

Average, marginal and total revenue

In Fig. 22 (see page 62) is a typical downward sloping demand curve which relates the quantity demanded at each price. This curve is constructed from the data in Table 13 (see page 62).

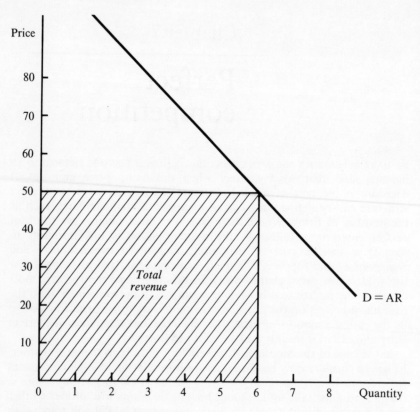

FIG 22: **Average and total revenue**

TABLE 13: **Total, average and marginal revenue**

Quantity (p)	Price (p)	Total revenue (TR=p×q)	Average revenue (TR÷q)	Marginal revenue
1	100	100	100	—
2	90	180	90	80
3	80	240	80	60
4	70	280	70	40
5	60	300	60	20
6	50	300	50	0
7	40	280	40	–20
8	30	240	30	–40

The first thing we note from Table 13 is that total revenue is price multiplied by the quantity purchased. Geometrically, it is the area of the box formed by a point on the demand curve, such as the shaded area in

Fig. 22. This revenue first rises but then begins to fall (after 6 units have been purchased). Second, average revenue is total revenue divided by the quantity purchased. Thus

$$\text{average revenue} = \frac{\text{total revenue}}{\text{quantity}} = \frac{\text{price} \times \text{quantity}}{\text{quantity}} = \text{price}$$

and is equal to the price. This means that if we plot average revenue against quantity, we are simply re-drawing the demand curve. This is true in all cases: the demand curve is also the average revenue curve.

Marginal revenue, like marginal cost, is less straightforward. Marginal revenue is the additional revenue received by selling one more unit. Thus, in order for the firm to raise sales from 3 units to 4 units it must lower the price from $80 to $70. Although total revenue rises from $240 to $280 the additional revenue received is only $40. This additional revenue is the marginal revenue of the fourth unit. If we plot average revenue, marginal revenue and total revenue against quantity we observe a number of important interrelationships. This is done in Fig. 23 (see page 64).

First, total revenue reaches its maximum when marginal revenue (MR) is zero. This should not be too surprising. So long as marginal revenue is positive then increasing sales will always add something to total revenue. When, however, marginal revenue is negative then each additional sale is reducing total revenue. Total revenue must therefore reach a maximum when marginal revenue is zero.

Second, marginal revenue is always less than average revenue (AR) when demand is downward sloping.

Third, for quantities below 6 units the elasticity of demand is greater than unity (i.e. elastic) while for quantities above 6 units it is less than unity (i.e. inelastic). At 6 units the elasticity is unity. (This cannot, however, be shown by the figures in going from 5 to 6 units.) To see this important point about elastic and inelastic demand, let us take two examples:

Example 1

Sales rising from 3 to 4 units.

$$\frac{(4-3)\times100}{3} \div \frac{(80-70)\times100}{80} = \frac{100}{3} \div \frac{100}{8} = 2\tfrac{2}{3}$$

Example 2

Sales rising from 7 to 8 units.

$$\frac{(8-7)\times100}{7} \div \frac{(40-30)\times100}{40} = \frac{100}{7} \div \frac{100}{4} = \frac{4}{7}$$

The first example shows that section of the demand curve to be elastic, while the second example shows that section of the demand curve to be inelastic. This result is most useful because it will be noted from Fig. 23

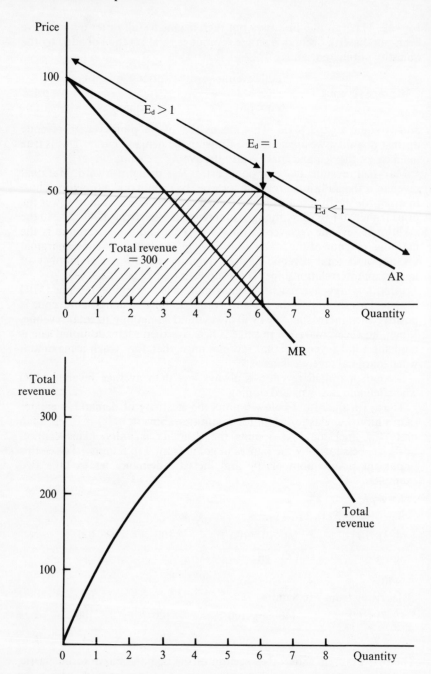

FIG. 23: **Interrelationships between average, marginal and total revenue**

that for a fall in price (a rise in quantity) above $50, total revenue rises. Thus, when demand is price elastic a fall in price is associated with a rise in total revenue. However, for a fall in price (a rise in quantity) below $50, total revenue falls. Thus, when demand is inelastic a fall in price leads to a fall in total revenue. The opposite is true for a rise in the price. Consequently, knowledge about the elasticity of demand will supply information about the change in total revenue.

What is the relationship between average revenue, marginal revenue and total revenue when demand is infinitely elastic; i.e. when the demand curve is horizontal at some fixed price? This we shall leave to the reader. Let the price be $80 and let this price be constant for all quantities sold. Construct a similar table to Table 13 and show that these results are true:

(1) average revenue = marginal revenue = price
(2) total revenue is a straight line through the origin.

Profit maximization under perfect competition

So far, we have established that under perfect competition the firm faces a fixed price. It is one of many firms which cannot influence any other. The demand curve for its output, then, is a horizontal straight line at the market determined price. This demand curve is also the average revenue curve *and* the marginal revenue curve.

But in order to consider *profits* we must first include costs as well as revenue. First we must say something about profits. Managements engage in risk-taking. They employ land, labour and capital in combination to produce an output which they hope to sell. (There is a difficulty in the treatment of management – or entrepreneurship. Either it can be treated as another factor of production and distinguished from other forms of labour; or, it can be considered not as a factor of production, but rather as the decision-maker who decides the quantity and combination of the factors of production.) Just as labour receives a wage for services rendered, so management receives a payment for undertaking management and risk. This return to management we call *normal profits*. Normal profits are part of costs, just as the wage bill or the expenditure on capital is part of costs. The point is that a manager could employ himself in some wage-earning occupation, but chooses not to. The return for not doing so is his income, which economists call normal profits. Such normal profits are, therefore, part of costs.

Profits, on the other hand, are simply the difference between total revenue and total costs:

profits = total revenue – total cost

If total revenue is equal to total costs, profits are zero. In other words, *supranormal profits* (profits over-and-above normal profits) are zero. If total revenue exceeds total costs then the firm is making a loss which is separate from its normal profits.

We made the point in Chapter 4 that a firm may have a number of objectives of which profit maximization is just one. Let us assume it is the only objective of the firm. The question we want to ask is: at what level of output will a firm's profits be maximized?

In order to answer this question we need to remind ourselves that marginal cost is the addition to total cost of producing one more unit of

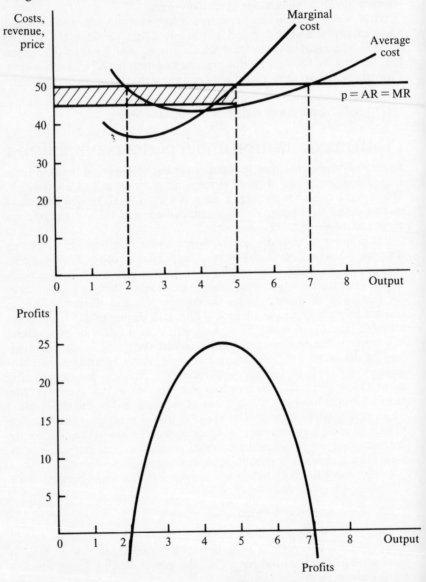

FIG. 24: **Profit maximization under perfect competition**

output. Marginal revenue is the addition to total revenue of selling one more unit. It follows, then, that if the additional cost of producing one more unit is less than the additional revenue from selling one more unit then profits will be increased by producing and selling one more unit. Thus, if

marginal cost < marginal revenue

then profits are rising. If, on the other hand, marginal cost is greater than marginal revenue then the additional cost of an extra unit is greater than the extra revenue received from selling it. Thus, if

marginal cost > marginal revenue

then profits are falling.

It follows, therefore, that profits must reach a maximum when marginal cost equals marginal revenue. Thus, profits are maximized if

marginal cost = marginal revenue

It is useful to see this result diagramatically. This is done in terms of Fig. 24. The firm is in a perfectly competitive market so that it faces a horizontal demand curve at, say, price $50. This curve also denotes the average revenue and marginal revenue curve. On the same diagram we have drawn the firm's average and marginal cost curves (which we discussed in Chapter 4).

Profits are at a maximum when marginal cost equals marginal revenue. Thus the firm should produce at output level of 5 units. If it produces 4 units then marginal revenue exceeds marginal cost and so the firm would be forgoing extra revenue in excess of the extra cost. It would be forgoing additional profits. If it produces in excess of 5 units then the additional cost would exceed the additional revenue and it would not be worthwhile for the firm to do so.

The output decision has been made. To maximize profits the firm must produce 5 units – or, more generally, at that level of output at which marginal cost is equal to marginal revenue. But we have yet to calculate what this level of profit is.

To do this it is convenient to consider profits in terms of average cost and average revenue. This is possible because average cost (AC) is total cost (TC) divided by output (q); while average revenue (AR) is total revenue (TR) divided by output (q). Thus,

$$
\begin{aligned}
\text{profits} &= \text{total revenue} - \text{total cost} \\
&= \frac{\text{total revenue}}{\text{output}} \times \text{output} - \frac{\text{total cost}}{\text{output}} \times \text{output} \\
&= \frac{\text{average}}{\text{revenue}} \times \text{output} - \frac{\text{average}}{\text{cost}} \times \text{output} \\
&= (\text{Average Revenue} - \text{Average Cost}) \times \text{Output}
\end{aligned}
$$

Thus, profits are the difference between average revenue and average cost multiplied by the level of output. This is shown in Fig. 24 by the shaded area. In this figure, average revenue equals price and is therefore equal to $50. Average cost is $45. Hence,

profits = ($50 − $45) × 5 = $25

Notice that where the average cost curve cuts the demand curve (or average revenue curve) then profits are zero. Thus the profits curve in the lower part of Fig. 24 cuts the output axis at 2 units, rises to a maximum at 5 units and thereafter falls, becoming zero again at 7 units.

Other objectives

Notice how important is the assumption of profit maximization. This assumption enables us to say exactly how much the firm should produce: this being determined where marginal cost equals marginal revenue. Suppose the firm was not a profit maximizer. Suppose, on the contrary, that it was happy to earn just $20, then any level of output between 3 units and 6 units would accomplish this. In this case the output level is indeterminate, although it must lie in the range 3 to 6 units. This is what the economist Herbert Simon refers to as a *satisficer*: the firm is satisfied with at least $20 of profits.

Why a firm may not maximize profits is complex. It is most usually because it also has other objectives which it is simultaneously trying to achieve, such as growth or market share.

The present example also illustrates an objective discussed by the economist, Baumol. He assumes that firms (especially oligopolists) wish to increase output as much as possible subject only to a minimum profit constraint. Suppose this profit constraint is $20. Then the firm in Fig. 24 will produce at 6 units. Notice two things about this result. First, it is a determinate solution in the sense that only one output level satisfies this (3 units minimizes rather than maximizes output). Second, it is not generally a profit maximizing position. Why should a firm do this? Why should it forgo profits? One possible reason is that it may wish to secure its market share. With greater sales its share of the market will be larger. But this takes us into the realm of oligopoly where market share becomes very important.

Perfect competition: long run solution

Let us return to the situation in Fig. 24 and re-drawn in part in Fig. 25. The market, shown in part (b) of Fig. 25 determines the price. Initially this is at $50. In this situation the firm is earning supranormal profits to the amount of $25. But this denotes profits over-and-above normal profits. It will therefore be attractive for firms to enter the industry to obtain some of these profits.

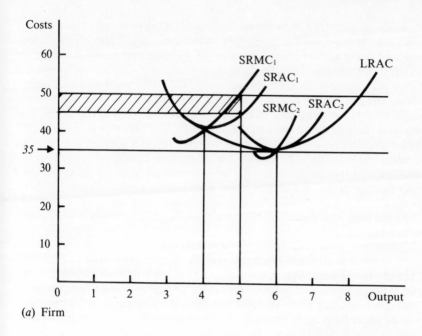

(a) Firm

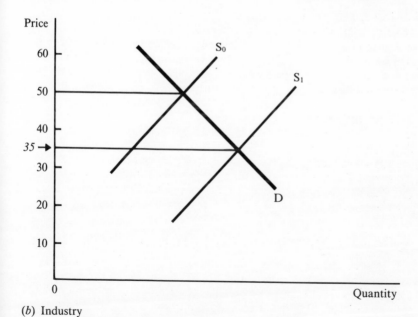

(b) Industry

FIG. 25: **Long run profit maximization under perfect competition**

As firms enter the industry so the market supply curve moves to the right. As it does so the price falls. Since this price also denotes the demand curve for the firm (equal to the average and marginal revenue curves), so this too falls. So long as supranormal profits are positive, firms will continue to enter the industry. They will cease to enter when there are no longer any supranormal profits. This is where the new demand curve is tangential to the *long run* average cost curve where the marginal cost cuts average cost. In terms of Fig. 25 (*a*) this is at price \$35 and output level of 6 units. Since at 6 units long run average cost equals average revenue then it follows that long run total cost equals total revenue and that long run profits are accordingly zero. In other words, only normal profits are earned in the long run by a perfectly competitive firm.

In the long run, therefore, the profit maximizing solution is where the firm is earning only normal profits.

Notice one important implication of this result. Since in the long run only normal profits are being earned the firm is operating at optimal capacity in the sense that it is operating at an output level at which long run average cost is a minimum. This is the appeal of perfect competition. With perfect entry and exit from the industry any supranormal profits will be short-lived and firms will operate eventually at minimum average cost.

Chapter 8

Monopoly

A MONOPOLIST IS A SINGLE PRODUCER of a commodity. As such he does not have to consider the behaviour of other firms. His behaviour is limited only by what consumers are prepared to accept. There is no such thing as a perfect monopolist; for such a thing to occur would require that it obtains all of a consumer's income. Since this is not so, a consumer can always switch his expenditure. Even state monopolies, such as, in some countries, coal or gas supplies are only one form of fuel and there is always some degree of substitutability.

This means that the demand curve facing a monopolist is the market demand curve and that it is downward sloping. Such a curve is shown in

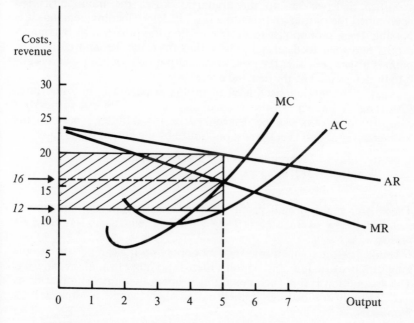

FIG. 26: **Monopoly**

Fig. 26. As we pointed out in Chapter 7, the demand curve is also the average revenue curve. Marginal revenue, however, no longer coincides with average revenue, as it did in perfect competition. With a downward sloping average revenue curve, marginal revenue is below average revenue, as shown in Fig. 26.

What output and price does a monopolist choose? In order to answer this question we must once again make an assumption about the firm's objective. We assume that the monopolist wishes to maximize his profits. Given this assumption, the firm will equate marginal revenue with marginal cost – just as in the case of perfect competition. This is always the rule for a profit-maximizing firm, regardless of the market structure. In terms of Fig. 26 this will require the firm to produce 5 units of output. Any less than 5 units or any more than 5 units will mean a lower level of profits than that associated with 5 units of output.

Can the monopolist set any price it wishes? The answer is, 'No'. If the monopolist sets a price higher than $20 then he cannot sell all of the 5 units which he knows will maximize his profits. If he sells at a price lower than $20 then he will once again make less profits because he can sell the 5 units he has decided to produce at $20. He will therefore set a price of $20. This price is determined by the demand curve. This is what we mean when we say that a monopolist's behaviour is conditioned only by consumer demand.

Notice that we set up the argument where the monopolist first determined the output and then the price is determined by demand. It is possible for a monopolist to determine first the price which maximizes profits and then to determine the output from the demand curve. The point is he can set either the price or the output but not both. Always one is to be determined by the demand curve.

What is the monopolist's level of profits at output level 5 and price $20? This is shown by the shaded area in Fig. 26. As for perfect competition, profits can be determined by the difference between the average revenue and average cost multiplied by the output level. Thus,

profits = (average revenue - average cost) × output
= ($20 – $12) × 5
= $40

These are supranormal profits because normal profits are already included in the average cost. They are often referred to as *monopoly profits*.

Unlike perfect competition, such monopoly profits can persist into the long run. Because it is a monopolist there is no other firm in the industry. The assumption is that such monopoly profits cannot attract other firms into the industry because if they did so there would no longer be a monopoly.

A rise/fall in costs

In Fig. 27 we consider the result of a rise in costs, such as labour costs, to the monopolist. A rise in wage costs pushes up both average and marginal costs to AC_2 and MC_2 respectively. Since demand has remained unchanged then so too do the average revenue and marginal revenue curves. The higher marginal cost, curve MC_2, now cuts the marginal revenue at a higher point. Output falls and the price rises: in terms of Fig. 27, output falls to 4 units and the price rises to $22.

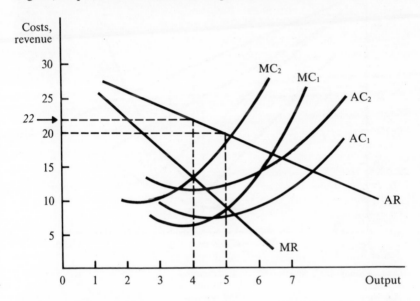

FIG. 27: **Monopolist's reaction to a rise in costs**

The same figure can be used to illustrate the effects of research and development. Suppose we begin with price at $22 and output at 4 units. In other words, suppose we begin with AC_2 and MC_2. The past accumulation of monopoly profits can be used to pay for research and development. Such research and development may prove successful and so lower costs. Thus, it may reduce average cost to AC_1 and marginal cost to MC_1. This results in a lower price, $20 instead of $22, and a greater output, 5 units in place of 4 units.

This possibility must always be kept in mind when criticizing monopolies. Under perfect competition supranormal profits are quickly wiped out and so these cannot be used for research and development. Of course, a monopolist may not use such profits for research and development. In which case these benefits will not occur.

An increase in demand

What is the result on a monopolist's price and output of an increase in demand? This is illustrated in Fig. 28. Costs throughout remain the same. The initial situation is given by average revenue AR_1 and marginal revenue MR_1. Price and output are determined where MR_1 equals marginal cost, in our illustration at price \$20 and output 5 units.

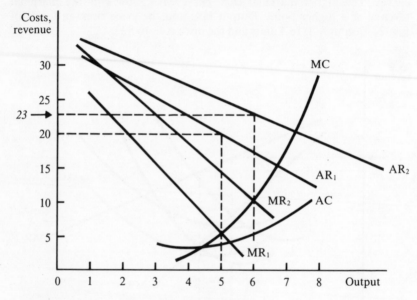

FIG. 28: **Monopolist's reaction to a rise in demand**

An increase in demand shifts the demand curve to AR_2 and also shifts marginal revenue to MR_2. The result in Fig. 28 is to raise the price to \$23 and raises the level of output to 6 units. This is not a general conclusion, however. Although an increase in demand will certainly raise the level of output, the price may rise, fall or remain the same. This is because there does *not* exist a market supply curve for a monopolist. Being the only supplier all price and output decisions are determined by the firm's marginal cost and marginal revenue in relation to the demand curve.

Discriminating monopoly

Consider a monopolist who can divide his market into two distinct groups. Examples are home sales and sales to overseas markets; first class and second class passengers; airline flights during the holiday season and out-of-season. In each of these examples the market demand in each category shows different characteristics. The most obvious difference is that they show different price elasticities of demand. For instance, the overseas market shows a greater price elasticity than the home market; first class passengers are not so responsive to price changes as are second class passengers; and in-season passengers are less responsive to price changes than out-of-season passengers. The question is: Should a monopolist charge the same price in both markets given this difference in demand elasticities?

The answer is, 'No'. To see why this is so, consider Fig. 29. Here there are two demand curves. The downward-sloping demand curve, with its associated marginal revenue curve, we assume is for the home market – and the curves are therefore labelled D^H and MR^H. Notice in particular that because demand is downward sloping then marginal revenue diverges from average revenue. On the other hand, the firm is assumed to operate in world markets in a perfectly competitive fashion, and so the foreign demand curve is horizontal at the world price of $5. In other words, the world demand curve D^F, equal to the world marginal revenue curve, MR^F, is horizontal. In this figure we have also drawn the firm's average and marginal costs.

First the firm must determine the total amount to produce for both markets combined. To determine this we first obtain the total marginal revenue for each level of output. At 3 units of output only the home market demands the good and at this output the marginal revenue is $10. From 5 units and above the firm can sell all it wishes to sell and so has a combined horizontal marginal revenue curve at $5. The combined marginal revenue curve is drawn as the thick kinked line. The firm will maximize profits by setting marginal cost equal to marginal revenue.

The firm will therefore produce 15 units of output. This output is, however, allocated to the two markets differently. Why is this? For a marginal cost of $5 then it is profitable to supply onto the home market 5 units (because at 5 units marginal revenue at home is equal to marginal cost). But the price is read off the home demand curve, and this price is $10. To summarize, home sales are 5 units and sales abroad are 10 units; the good is sold at home for $10 but at $5 overseas. The higher price is charged in the market with the smallest price elasticity of demand. This is the general result for a discriminating monopolist.

In the examples given this explains why the home market price is higher than that at which the same commodity is sold abroad; why first class fares are higher than second class fares; and why in-season flights are more expensive than out-of-season flights.

For discriminating monopoly to operate the two markets must be quite distinct and no re-sale must occur. To see why this is so, suppose goods are sold overseas at $5 and at home for $10, as in the situation shown in Fig. 29 (see page 76). It is possible for overseas buyers to re-sell the goods to the home market for, say, $7 (a process called *dumping*). In the case of in-season and out-of-season no problem arises because they are at different times of the year. With first and second class passengers re-sale is avoided by making the first class service better than the second class.

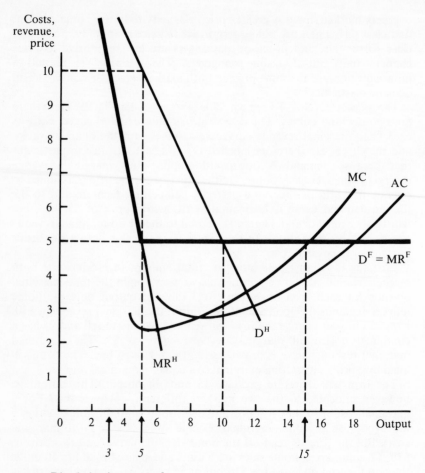

FIG. 29: Discriminating monopoly

Monopolistic competition

Monopolistic competition, as its name indicates, has features of both monopoly and competition. Strictly, it is a form of oligopoly in the sense that there is a number of firms in the industry. Unlike perfect competition, however, the firm does have some control over the market. This control comes from advertising. It is assumed that the firm differentiates its product, that is makes it sufficiently different from rival products. It does this through advertising. The purpose of the advertising is to achieve some form of brand loyalty. Coca-Cola, for example, is a drink which competes with other drinks. But it has a brand name and through advertising a company can attract a number of buyers who will repeatedly buy Coca-Cola in preference to similar drinks.

The monopoly feature of monopolistic competition is in having a market for a particular branded product. Unlike monopoly, however, other firms exist with similar branded products, e.g. Pepsi Cola as distinct from Coca-Cola. The demand curve for the firm is therefore downward sloping, as shown in Fig. 30.

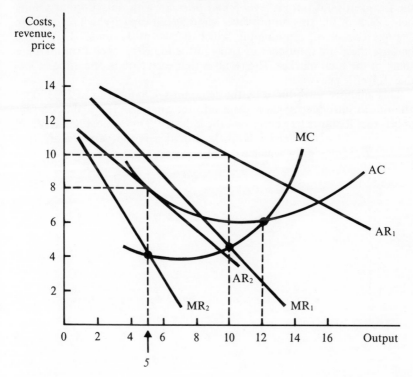

FIG. 30: **Monopolistic competition**

The initial situation is given by demand curve AR₁ with its associated marginal revenue curve MR₁. Since it aims to maximize profits it equates marginal cost with marginal revenue. It will accordingly produce 10 units and sell these for $10 each. Notice, that like monopoly the price is determined by the demand curve.

Unlike monopoly, however, firms can enter the industry. In the present illustration they will do so. This is because this firm is earning profits over-and-above normal profits. (These profits are the difference between average revenue and average cost multiplied by the output.) Firms will enter the industry. Demand will be spread across more firms and so this firm will lose some of its demand. The demand curve accordingly shifts to the left. It will continue to shift until all supranormal profits are eliminated. This is shown by demand curve AR₂ and its associated marginal revenue curve, MR_2. Notice that where MR_2 cuts the marginal cost curve, at output level 5 units, the price is just equal to the average cost. Average cost is equal to average revenue and so supranormal profits are zero.

One other implication can be seen in terms of Fig. 30. In the long run the firm settles at output level 5 and price $8 with only normal profits being earned. But this output level is not at full capacity, which is where average cost is at a minimum, which occurs at 12 units. This arises because there are a number of firms in the industry, each firm taking a share of the total market. The result is that each firm is operating at less than full efficiency.

This analysis, introduced by the economist, Chamberlin in 1933, does attempt to introduce some realism into the analysis. The main criticism of it is that it allows free entry into the industry. This is most unlikely and some form of entry barrier is likely. But this is the very feature that characterizes oligopoly, which we deal with next.

Chapter 9

Oligopoly

IN THE PREVIOUS TWO CHAPTERS we discussed the two extreme forms of product markets: perfect competition and monopoly. The former is characterized by many firms competing in such a way that no one of them has any influence over the price; the individual firm can sell as much as it wishes at the price determined by market demand and supply. In the case of monopoly the firm is the only supplier and is faced with a downward-sloping demand curve. It sets its price or its quantity in such a way as to equate marginal revenue with marginal cost because this will maximize its profits. *Oligopoly* refers to the market structure where a few firms compete. (If the number of firms is just two, then it is referred to as *duopoly*.) But the fact that there are just a few firms in the industry is not the main characteristic of oligopoly. The main feature of oligopoly is that the firm must take into account the reaction of its rivals to whatever it does. Also it has to take account of the behaviour of other firms in the industry. The fewness of numbers is a feature of this inter-dependence. It is the fact that there are a few firms which means each can influence the price in some way, but exactly how depends on how its rivals will react to its behaviour.

Because the main feature of oligopoly is the reaction of one firm to another, there is a variety of forms which oligopoly can take depending on the type of behaviour we assume. In this chapter we shall discuss just a few of these models of oligopoly and some of the characteristics of oligopoly situations.

Price leadership

One common form of oligopoly is where the dominant firm in the industry sets the price and other firms follow. In this situation the reaction of rivals is known. The dominant firm knows that the others in the industry will follow its lead, and the less dominant firms always follow the leader (and so each of the non-dominant firms reacts in the same way.) The inter-dependence is clear and the uncertainty to a large extent is eliminated.

The dominant firm is usually the biggest in the industry or the most efficient. The reason why other firms will follow the lead of the dominant firm is to prevent a price-cutting war. The feature of oligopoly is that with just a small number of firms in the industry it is possible for one firm to increase its market share if it can under-cut its rivals.

But such price-cutting is often defeatist because rivals will quite simply bring down their prices in response and so the relative positions of the firms will remain the same – but at the lower price. So in order to avoid such price wars firms agree to follow a leader. One international example of such price leadership is to be found in the oil industry. OPEC tends to be the price leader and Britain, which sells North Sea oil, is a price follower.

Where this situation may become a little unstable is where the leadership is contested: a firm which formerly was a follower may wish to become a leader. In this situation there is some price-cutting until leadership is established.

Another form of the price leadership model of oligopoly is called *barometric pricing*. (A barometer measures atmospheric pressure changes, and so the barometric firm is an indicator of changes in the market.) A barometric firm, therefore, is one which is sensitive to market conditions. It may not be the biggest firm in the industry, however, but it is the most sensitive to market conditions. This firm becomes the price leader. When it changes its price, other firms follow.

Collusive pricing

Another form of oligopoly is that of collusion. In this situation firms agree together on the price which will be set. Where collusion takes the form of an agreement the situation is referred to as a *cartel*. Consequently, the agreement between OPEC countries on the price at which oil will sell in world markets is a cartel. In some countries, most especially in Britain and the USA, cartels are illegal. Of course, this does not prevent firms having an informal agreement, which can be as effective as a formal one.

But why should firms collude, whether formally or informally? One reason is to prevent a price war, which we discussed previously. But in order to avoid a price war the agreement is aimed at maximizing the joint profits of the group. This is an important point. To maximize the joint profits does not imply that each firm is maximizing its profits. It is here where there is some instability in such collusive pricing. For example, one firm in the group feels it is more efficient allowing it to lower its costs, then by reducing its price it can increase its market share and its level of profits. Such behaviour will be less likely the more similar the firms are in terms of size, market share and the product that they produce.

Entry limit pricing

One special form of collusion is where firms already in the industry set an agreed price which either limits or prevents other firms from entering the industry – hence the term *entry limit pricing*. We noted that in perfect competition there is perfect entry and exit from the industry. Here this assumption is being violated by a deliberate act of policy.

In order to limit or prevent entry the price must be set sufficiently low to prevent firms from entering the industry and obtaining some of the supranormal profits which are being obtained. Firms, however, cannot set the price too low because they then may not be covering their costs and will make losses rather than profits. Limit pricing tends to arise when a firm prices its product based on its long-run situation, the aim being to maximize long-run profits. In this case it sets the price in relation to long-run costs. New firms entering the industry cannot possibly rival such already existing firms because it will take them many years to arrive at the same long-run situation. The extent to which firms can engage in limit pricing depends largely on the economies of scale in the industry. The greater the economies of scale the lower the long-run average costs and the lower the limit price that can be set by existing firms.

Full cost pricing

In perfect competition, price was set equal to marginal cost. In monopoly, price was set equal to average revenue, once the level of output had been determined by equating marginal revenue with marginal cost. Studies done on actual firms' behaviour found that firms generally set their price in the following way. The firm first determined the variable costs of producing a level of output. In other words, the cost of labour, raw materials, etc., divided by the level of output. It then added to this an amount to cover average fixed costs, such as rent, and a profit margin. This situation is shown in Fig. 31 (see page 82).

Notice that we have drawn the average variable cost curve as L-shaped. This is important. Once output is in the region where average variable costs become constant, then regardless of the level of output, the firm simply determines the average variable costs and adds a constant mark-up to cover average fixed costs and a profit margin.

Such oligopolistic behaviour does not take account of marginal revenue or marginal cost; the firm does not necessarily determine its output to achieve maximum profits and there is no obvious reference to demand. In particular, price is not determined by the interaction of demand and supply but is, on the contrary, determined by the firm. Consumers simply have to accept the price which is set. Even so, demand does play a role. Consider the demand curve drawn in Fig. 31. Here the price is determined by average revenue. We have drawn it in such a way that the mark-up and output are such that the price set is equal to average revenue at that level of sales. Given this demand curve, therefore, if the mark-up had been greater then sales would not have been as great as expected. If the mark-up was smaller then there are profits to be made even at the same level of output.

This theory also explains some features of growing sectors and declining sectors. An economy which is booming will have demand curves shifting to the right. This will allow two extreme possibilities: either increased sales with the same mark-up, or increased profits with the same sales. Since the studies indicated that, generally, firms kept mark-ups relatively constant, a boom led to increased sales. During a depression, however, the demand curve shifts to the left. In this situation the likely response is first to accept a declining profit margin, but then to reduce sales. Both increased profits during a boom and a fall in profits during a slump are very characteristic of oligopoly firms.

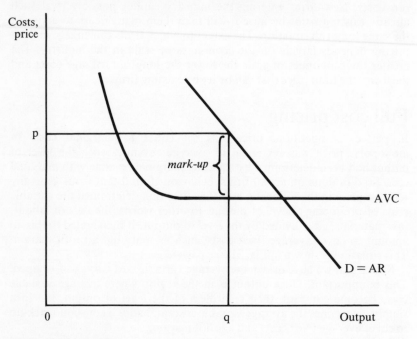

FIG. 31: **Full cost pricing**

The kinked demand curve

One feature of oligopoly in a number of countries has been the fact that prices are not changed very frequently. One theory to explain this has been the kinked demand curve. It is important to realize that this is not a theory about price determination, but rather a theory about the fixity of oligopoly prices.

The situation is shown in Fig. 32. We begin with a price p*, which is historically determined in some way. For this firm we make two different assumptions about its rivals' reactions when it changes its price. If it should lower its price then all firms will do the same. This gives rise to demand curve D_1. If it should raise its price, then other firms will not

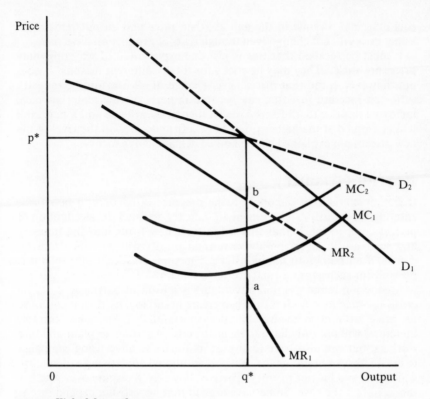

FIG. 32: Kinked demand curve

follow. This leads to demand curve D_2. Notice that D_2 is less steep than D_1 because not only will sales fall when the price rises, but it will also lose some of its market share when it raises the price because other firms will not follow it. On the other hand, when the price falls sales will increase, and because other firms are doing likewise there is no change in the relative market shares. Hence, D_1 is steeper than D_2. Also notice that D_1 applies only for prices below p^* while D_2 applies only for prices above p^*. Hence, the kink occurs at the price p^*.

To each of the demand curves there is an associated marginal revenue curve. However, marginal revenue MR_1 applies only for output levels above q^* (i.e. for prices below p^*) while marginal revenue MR_2 applies only for output levels below q^* (i.e. for prices above p^*). This means that at the output level q^* there is a 'gap' in the combined marginal revenue curves, shown by the vertical distance marked ab. Suppose, then, that marginal cost is MC_1, as shown in Fig. 32. If the firm is equating marginal revenue with marginal cost it will produce output level q^* and sell it at a price p^*. Now suppose the costs of production rise and marginal costs increase to MC_2, also shown in Fig. 32. Since MC_2 still cuts marginal revenue in the gap ab, then price and output remain the same. Prices do not change even though costs of production have risen.

It must be recalled that this is just one explanation of why oligopoly prices are sticky. They may be sticky for totally different reasons. It does not, however, mean that prices never change. If all firms in the industry suffer an increase in costs, say because imports of raw materials have increased in price to all firms equally, then price will rise and a new kink will be formed at the higher price. How a firm decides on the level of the new price is not explained by the kinked demand curve theory.

Barriers to entry

One characteristic of oligopoly is the presence of barriers to new firms entering the industry. If profits in an industry are high the assumption of perfect competition is that this will attract new firms into the industry and such profits over-and-above normal profits will be wiped out. Of course, if entrants into the industry are in some way kept out, then it is possible for such supranormal profits to remain.

A common remark is that advertising is a form of barrier to entry by creating *brand loyalty*. If a firm can create brand loyalty then it can raise its price without reducing its sales substantially. Any new entrant, therefore, will not only have to incur the cost of setting up plant and hire workers, but will also have to engage in a massive advertising campaign to create its own brand image. It is this additional advertising expenditure which acts as a barrier to entry. There is, however, a dispute over whether this is in fact the case. Some have argued that advertising expenditure is not so much directed at creating a brand image, but rather at attempting to attract consumers away from rival brands to their own. If this is true, then advertising, far from being a barrier to entry, is in fact a means of competition – both for existing firms and for new potential entrants.

Another entry barrier is that of absolute cost. Existing firms may be able to use techniques not available to new entrants and also they have established customer relations with other firms supplying them with inputs and finance. It means that existing firms can obtain lower prices for their raw materials, and finance may be cheaper or discounts greater.

A third barrier to entry is caused by economies of scale. This we have mentioned, but is clarified further in Fig. 33. The minimum efficient scale for this firm is assumed to be 10 units and at this output level unit costs are $5. The market has a demand of 40 units and so will cater for 4 minimum efficient-scale plants. Suppose there are 4 such firms already operating. A new entrant will have to produce at a level of output below the minimum efficient scale. Even if the new entrant has the same cost curve as that shown in Fig. 33, it will still have a much higher cost than $5 and so it would have to charge a price higher than that of a firm already in the industry. The more steeply falling the average cost curve, the greater the entry barrier arising from economies of scale.

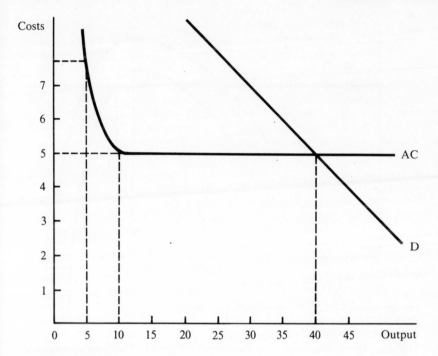

FIG. 33: **Barrier to entry**

A fourth entry barrier arises from the presence of patents and copyrights. (A patent gives a person or firm the sole right for a period of time to make, use or sell, some invention; while a copyright gives exclusive rights to an author or designer for a number of years to make copies of or give performances of his original work.) Although these also occur under monopoly they are probably more significant in oligopoly. By having a patent or copyright a firm has legal limited access to an invention or material for the period of the agreement.

Baumol's Theory of Sales Revenue Maximization

One observation in the real world did not appear to be verified by the perfect competition model or the model of monopoly: namely, when a tax on profits occurred firms did alter their output. Since a profits tax neither alters marginal revenue nor marginal cost then it does not alter the profit-maximizing output level or the price set. What it does is simply reduce the level of profits at this position. However, in the real world oligopolistic firms tended to reduce their output when a profits tax was imposed.

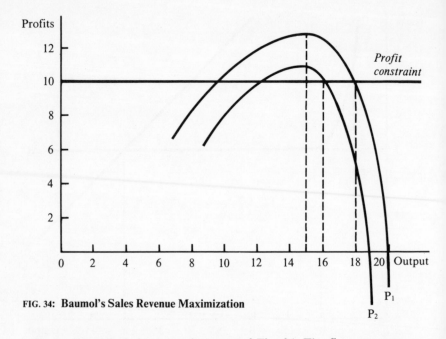

FIG. 34: Baumol's Sales Revenue Maximization

Baumol's analysis is shown in terms of Fig. 34. The firm attempts to achieve a maximum revenue sales subject to a minimum profit constraint. The initial profits curve is given by P_1 and the profit constraint is $10. In Fig. 34 we note the following observations:

1. The profit maximizing output level is 15 units
2. The sales revenue maximizing output level (with no profit constraint) is 20 units
3. With a minimum profit margin of $10, the sales revenue maximizing output level is 18 units.

Now suppose a profits tax is imposed lowering the profits curve to P_2. Then we note the following results:

1. The profit maximizing level is still 15 units
2. The sales revenue maximizing output level (with no profit constraint) is 19 units
3. With a minimum profit margin of $10, the sales revenue maximizing output level is 16 units.

Although this theory of oligopoly does explain some of the observations we see in the real world, especially about advertising, it gives no explanation of the minimum profit constraint.

Managerial and behavioural theories of the firm

It will be noted that in the last model of oligopoly we moved away from profit maximization as a goal of the firm. When this is done we enter a realm of models which have been called 'managerial models'. The attempt in these models has been to specify more clearly the possible objectives that managements have.

One of the very early models was that of the economist, Marris (see 'Further Reading'). He began with the observation that a firm in a modern market economy is not privately owned but is a limited company with shareholders. The company is run by a manager or board of directors. Their aim is not necessarily to maximize profits, although profits are not totally neglected. Marris argued that the objective was in fact to maximize the rate of growth of the firm. Such growth is constrained in two important respects. First, by the expertise of the management team. Second, by the fact that managers wish to maximize their job security. (Why maximize profits when that goes to shareholders!) Of course, job security for the manager is not independent of the level of profits. A firm with little or no profits will lead the shareholders to dispense with the services of the manager!

This model was just the first in a series of managerial models which attempted to bring into the analysis the modern corporation with its division between ownership (the shareholders) and control (management). In simple terms, they all attempt to define a series of objectives which are pursued by managers in running large corporations.

At the same time, a slightly different approach was taken by behaviourists, such as Cyert and March. They based their analysis on the fact that firms are (*a*) multiproduct (i.e. produce more than one product), (*b*) operate in a world of uncertainty, and (*c*) operate in an imperfectly competitive market. Like the managerial theories, these begin with the division between ownership and control. But they develop along different lines. The difference comes from the behaviourists seeing the internal workings of the large corporation as a problem in decision-making. Put another way, two firms can be faced with the same external stimuli (such as a profits tax) but react quite differently because they go about making decisions in a different way. In order, therefore, to investigate oligopoly reactions behaviourists look at the internal decision-making of the firm.

Conclusion

It will be noted that we have mentioned a lot of theories about oligopoly (and there are many more). None of them explains all of the imperfectly competitive behaviour which we observe in the real world. Each theory has something to offer to our understanding, but none is comprehensive. But then there is no reason why there should be only one model of imperfect competition. Just because we give this form of competition a name by calling it 'imperfect competition' does not necessarily mean that any single form of it exists in the real world. In all probability there will be many forms and we shall require many theories of oligopolistic behaviour.

Chapter 10

Factor markets

SO FAR WE HAVE BEEN CONCERNED WITH a firm's output and price decision. In order to produce this output a manager must combine his plant, machines, labour, etc. These are generally classified as *factor inputs*. For purposes of our discussion we can consider just two: labour and capital. We can think of capital comprising the plant and machines which are combined with labour to produce output.

Given that a manager knows his output and his price, the question arises: How much labour and capital should he use? In this chapter we shall concentrate on the firm's demand for labour. The demand for capital follows a similar argument. Basically, we want to know what determines the demand for labour and what determines the wage rate. Put generally, we want to know what determines the demand for a factor of production (land, labour and capital) and the factor price (rent, wages and the return on capital).

When we consider the market economy outlined in Fig. 2, it was households which demanded goods and services and it was firms that supplied these goods and services. When we turn to factors of production, it is households which supply these factors and it is firms that demand them. This opposite flow is important. By households supplying their labour they receive payment for their services as wages and salaries. By supplying firms with some of their savings they receive interest payments. By supplying land they receive rent. These factor incomes are the source of income households have for purchasing goods and services. Such a circular flow of income is the basis of national income accounting.

One other feature of factor demand is important. Labour is not demanded for itself, as is the case with, say, food. Labour is demanded because when it is combined with other factors of production it can be used to produce some commodity. It is the commodity which is being demanded for itself. Consequently, labour is a *derived demand*. In fact, if there was no demand for the good then a firm would not be demanding any factor input. Consequently, the demand for any factor of production is a derived demand.

The firm's output and price is determined in the case where the objective of the firm is to maximize profits. However, the demand for labour does not depend only on the assumption of profit maximization, but also on the type of competition the firm is involved in.

The two extremes are perfect competition and monopoly. But these are with respect to the firm's output. It is possible for a firm to be the only firm requiring a particular type of labour. In this case we have a *monopsonist*: a single buyer. More generally, many firms will be demanding factors of production, and we can assume a situation of perfect competition in the factor market. This assumption requires not only many firms demanding factors of production, but that factor services are not restricted in any way. Labour, for example, is assumed not to be organized into large unions. If labour is organized into large unions and if there is only a limited number of firms demanding such unionized labour then we have a situation of *oligopsony*. In this chapter we shall deal only with the situation of perfect competition in the factor market, although we shall allow both perfect competition and monopoly in the product market.

Average and marginal products

Throughout this book we have repeatedly made use of the concepts of average and marginal. It will be recalled that a profit-maximizing firm determines its output by equating marginal cost with marginal revenue; that a firm's profit is determined by the difference between average revenue and average cost multiplied by the level of output; that consumers base their demands on marginal utility. Similar concepts are involved in determining a firm's demand for a factor of production. This is why it is called the *marginal productivity theory of factor demand*.

Let us concentrate on labour and hold capital constant. Now if we increase labour input then output will increase. The total output, or total product of labour, will vary as labour varies. The situation is shown in Table 14 and in Fig. 35 (see page 91).

TABLE 14: **Total, average and marginal physical products of labour**

Labour (L)	Total physical product of labour (TPP$_L$)	Average physical product of labour (APP$_L$)	Marginal physical product of labour (MPP$_L$)
1	10	10	—
2	24	12	14
3	42	14	18
4	52	13	10
5	60	12	8
6	66	11	6
7	70	10	4

The *average physical product of labour* is derived by dividing the total product of labour by the number of labour units used to produce this output (also known as labour productivity). Thus,

Average physical product of labour $= \dfrac{\text{total product}}{\text{labour input}}$

The *marginal physical product of labour* is the additional output obtained from employing one more (or one less) unit of labour. Thus, in going from 3 units of labour to 4 units of labour total output rises from 42 to 52 units. The fourth unit of labour adds an additional 10 units to output.

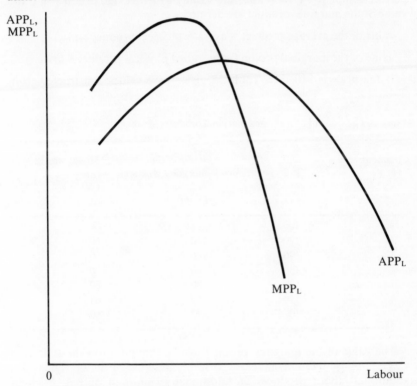

FIG. 35: **Average and marginal physical products of labour**

Notice that all these figures refer to physical quantities. The reason why average and marginal physical products of labour eventually decline is that labour is being used with a fixed factor. Imagine a firm with just one workshop. As labour is first increased output will increase rapidly, but there comes a point when all machines are fully used. Additional labour will simply get in each others' way. Although output may rise it will probably not rise by as much as before. In other words, the marginal physical product of labour begins to decline. Soon the average physical product also declines. We in fact discussed this in Chapter 4 and referred to it as diminishing returns to labour as a result of other factor inputs being held constant.

To use these concepts we must first convert them into values. But we must be very careful here. Under perfect competition in the product market (i.e. the market where the firm sells its output) the price remains constant regardless of how many units are sold. As labour is increased, therefore, the average physical product always sells for the same price and the marginal physical product is always priced the same. Under perfect competition, therefore, the value of the average product and the value of the marginal product are defined:

value of the average product = average physical product × price

value of the marginal product = marginal physical product × price

If the price is $10 then Table 15 gives these values constructed from Table 14.

TABLE 15: **The value of average and marginal products of labour**

Labour (L)	Value of the average product of labour (VAP$_L$)	Value of the marginal product of labour (VMP$_L$)	Money wage rate (W)
1	100	—	60
2	120	140	60
3	140	180	60
4	130	100	60
5	120	80	60
6	110	60	60
7	100	40	60

The value of the marginal product can be thought of in the following way. Suppose labour increases from 3 units to 4 units. Then this additional labour produces an additional 10 units of output. Each of these is sold for $10 each, and so the value of this output is $100. Thus, the value to the firm of employing the fourth unit of labour is $100.

What is the situation where the firm sells its product in a market where the demand curve is downward sloping? We know that with a downward sloping demand curve the price is equal to the average revenue curve. But more importantly, the marginal revenue is *less* than the average revenue. (A look back at Fig. 23 will help.) This means that each unit is sold with a different marginal revenue. In this case we talk of the *average revenue product* of labour (ARP$_L$) and the *marginal revenue product* of labour (MRP$_L$). These are defined as:

average revenue product = average physical product × marginal revenue

marginal revenue product = marginal physical product × marginal revenue

To see why this is so consider once again raising labour from 3 units to 4 units. This leads to an increase in output of 10 units. But each of these 10 units brings in only an additional revenue given by the marginal revenue. Thus, we must multiply the marginal physical product by the marginal revenue rather than by the price. The same applies to the average physical revenue. These are shown in Fig. 36.

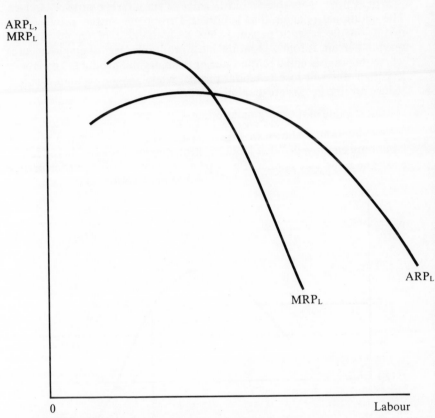

FIG. 36: **Average and marginal revenue products of labour**

With these concepts now clarified we can turn to the demand for labour.

The demand for labour

Let us first take the situation of perfect competition in both the product market and the factor market. This means each output is sold at the one price and all labour is employed at the same wage. Suppose the wage is $60. If the firm is to maximize profits what amount of labour will it demand?

The information is contained in Table 15. Suppose the firm employs 2 units of labour. Then the value of the output produced by this second unit of labour will be $140 while it costs the firm only $60 in wages for this extra unit of labour. It would be profitable for the firm to hire this second unit of labour. Similarly, the third unit leads to $180 additional revenue and to a cost of only $60. So this too would be profitable.

Would it be profitable to hire 7 units of labour? The answer is, 'No'. The additional revenue that is obtained from the output produced by taking on the seventh person is less than the cost of employing that seventh person. It follows that the most profitable level of employment is where the wage is equal to the value of the marginal product. Any labour less than this will lose potential profits, while any more than this will reduce profits. Profits are maximized where

wage = value of the marginal product.

The situation is shown in Fig. 37. At a wage of $60 then 6 units of labour are employed. What labour is demanded if the wage should fall to $40? The same rule applies. For a profit-maximizing firm under perfect

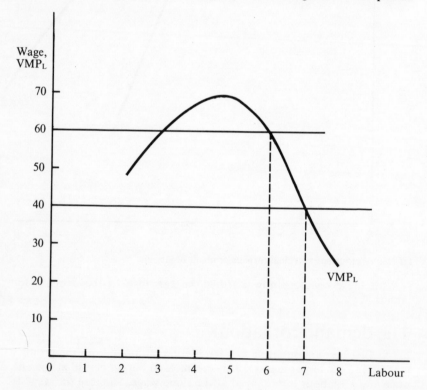

FIG. 37: **Demand for labour**

competition in the product and factor markets, the wage is equated with the value of the marginal product. Hence, 7 units of labour are demanded.

It will be noted that the labour demanded at each wage is read off from the value of the marginal product. This curve is, therefore, the demand curve for labour.

The situation where there is a downward sloping demand curve for the product is only slightly different. In this case the wage is equated with the marginal revenue product. The marginal revenue product curve is the demand curve for labour by the firm.

Since both the value of the marginal product declines and the marginal revenue product declines, the demand curve for labour by a firm also declines. In other words, we have a downward sloping demand curve for labour, as shown in Fig. 38. The same result occurs no matter which factor of production we are considering. The demand for a factor of production rises as its price falls.

Although we have derived the demand curve for the firm, the result is

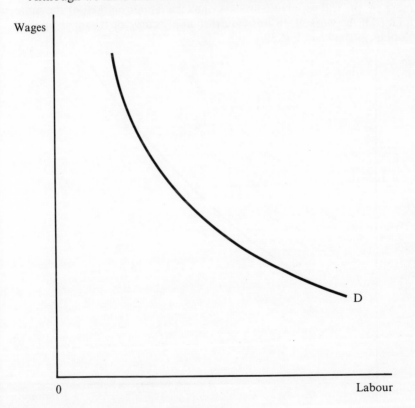

FIG. 38: A firm's demand curve for labour

also true for the market as a whole: the market demand curve for labour is downward sloping. When the wage falls, firms as a whole will demand more labour and when the wage rises firms will demand less labour.

The supply of labour

So far we have considered what determines the demand for labour. The other side of the market is the supply of labour. The supply of labour is not simply the working population. In some societies this may include women, but in others only to a limited extent are women included. When considering a particular occupation the supply will also depend on the age and skill of the population. The wage too is an important factor in determining the supply of labour.

If we hold all factors like age, sex and skill of the population constant, we can consider the supply curve of labour as representing the wage in relation to the number of persons supplying themselves for work (or the number of man-hours) at that wage. Generally, the greater the wage the more people will supply themselves onto the labour market, or the more hours will be worked. In this case the supply curve of labour is upward sloping, as shown in Fig. 39.

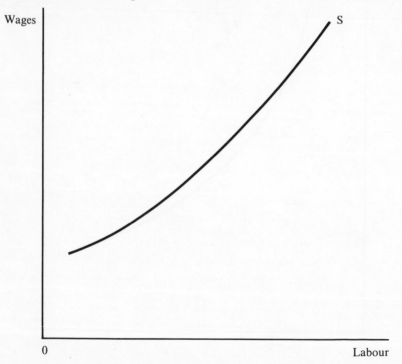

FIG. 39: **Market supply curve of labour**

It must be realized that for most societies work is not in itself rewarding. Wages are paid in order to attract someone to work. In other words, wages are the payment to forgo 'leisure'. Leisure does not here mean idleness, but rather all those things a person would like to do in a non-work situation. Of course, many of the things a person would like to do involve the purchase of goods and services, and so a person will work in order to earn an income to pay for such goods and services.

It is possible that at a certain 'high' wage, income is sufficiently high to pursue even more leisure activities and that at higher wages still a person may even reduce the hours worked. In this case the supply curve of labour may be backward bending. This possibility has not been convincingly demonstrated for developed countries, and for many developing countries the population is such that the supply curve can be thought of as horizontal – that is, an infinitely elastic supply of labour. This would arise at a wage at or close to the subsistence wage.

Economic rent

Like all supply curves, the wage read off from the supply curve is the minimum price that that factor is prepared to accept in order to supply itself onto the market. But suppose the price it actually receives is higher than this. Look at Fig. 40. Five units of labour are prepared to let

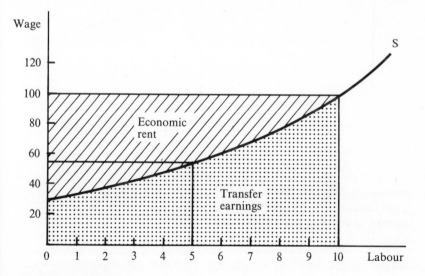

FIG. 40: **Economic rent**

themselves be hired for $55, but in fact they get paid $100. This is because all units are paid the same. The gap between what a factor is prepared to accept and what he is actually paid is referred to as *economic rent*.

The wage that a person is prepared to accept is often called his *transfer earnings*, in the sense that it denotes the minimum necessary to attract that person from some other job or occupation and into the present one. Thus, economic rent is the area above the supply curve and below the wage line; while transfer earnings is the area below the supply curve.

To illustrate the importance of economic rent consider a totally inelastic supply curve for some factor of production – such as labour or land – as shown in Fig. 41.

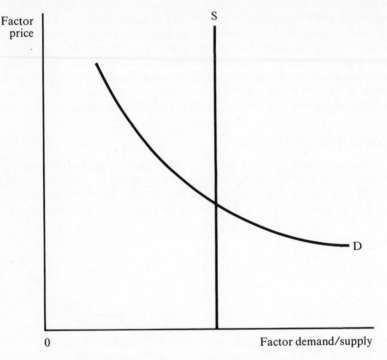

FIG. 41: **Totally inelastic supply of a factor of production**

Two things are important about this. First, the price of the factor is determined solely by the demand for it. A greater demand (a demand curve further to the right) would mean a higher factor price; a smaller demand (a demand curve further to the left) would mean a lower factor price. Thus, if this was the market for a film star or pop star then the more popular that star the greater the demand for his or her performance and the greater the wage. This is why some film and pop stars earn very high wages – but those high wages last only so long as their popularity lasts. Similarly, if some particular piece of land is in an ideal location, then its supply is limited. The rent for such land (in the normal use of the word rent) is also very high.

Second, the more inelastic the supply curve for a factor of production the greater the economic rent and the smaller the transfer earnings. In the extreme case shown in Fig. 41, *all* the factor price denotes economic rent. The reason for this can be understood by returning to our example of a pop star. A particular pop star is unique. If there were no demand there would be no price for her performance. Put another way, if the person wishes to perform she will accept whatever price she can get. (Pop stars frequently begin their careers accepting very low wages for their performances in the hope and expectation of being a success in the future.)

An important policy implication of the distinction between a factor price and transfer earnings is that economic rent can be taxed without any change in market behaviour. This is because economic rent, as its name implies, is over-and-above what the person is prepared to accept. Any taxing of this rent, therefore, simply lowers the windfall gain. Such tax is quite common on land rents for city property where high demand raises the price and leads to capital gains by property owners. The difficulty in doing this lies in estimating what part of a factor price is economic rent and what part is a transfer earning.

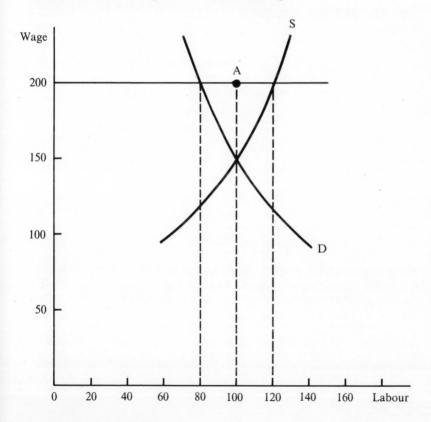

FIG. 42: **Market-determined wage**

Wage rates

Factor prices are determined by the interplay of demand and supply. If we return to labour as a typical example, then the *equilibrium wage* is where the demand for labour equals the supply of labour: at wage $150 in Fig. 42. At this wage 100 people wish to work and firms are demanding 100 people.

Suppose, however, that the government sets a *minimum wage* of $200. In this case firms are demanding only 80 people while at this wage 120 people wish to work. This means 40 people must go involuntarily unemployed. This is a disequilibrium situation which will likely cause problems in the future.

Another disequilibrium situation is also illustrated in Fig. 42. Suppose there exists a powerful trade union which negotiates a wage/employment situation shown by point A. In other words, even though demand and supply are as shown by the two curves, the trade union gets agreement for the firm to hire 100 workers at a wage of $200. This leads to over-manning in the sense that the firm wishes to employ only 80 but hires 100. This too can lead to problems in the future.

Chapter 11

Efficiency and competition

TWO OF THE MOST FUNDAMENTAL CONCEPTS in microeconomics are those of efficiency and competition. We shall discuss both of these in this chapter. Our intention is to discuss exactly what is meant by efficiency (and hence inefficiency) and by competition. One of the reasons for dealing with them more thoroughly is that economists discuss different kinds of efficiency and there are also different forms of competition – the most obvious being price competition and non-price competition.

Not all of the aspects affecting efficiency and competition are covered in the models outlined in this book. For a fuller view, it would be necessary to follow the continuing debate about how far our understanding of firms can be built upon observation and analysis of conduct and performance. Scherer's book, *Industrial Market Structure and Economic Performance*, sets out this debate in some detail. Organizational theories in particular consider the internal organization of the firm and view conduct and performance from an organizational perspective. In these theories management and labour have individual objectives which may be inconsistent with profit maximization. Furthermore, such theories link the concepts of efficiency and competition, as we shall show below.

Efficiency

In Chapter 4, on the firm, production and costs, we introduced the concept of efficiency. There we said that *technical efficiency* is producing a given output with a given technology with the minimum of factor inputs. Or, given the level of inputs and technology, technical efficiency refers to the maximum output that is obtainable. The reason why this is referred to as technical efficiency is that it does not consider factor prices nor does it consider organization.

When account is taken of factor prices (but not organization) then we have *economic efficiency*, which means that for a given technology and a given level of output a firm is economically efficient if it combines its factor inputs so as to produce this output at the lowest possible cost. One way to view economic efficiency is to realize that for a firm to be economically efficient it must be *on* its average cost curve when assessing costs. For instance, in Fig. 43, 5 units of output can be produced at $10. Suppose, however, that the firm is over-manned and has more labour

102 · Efficiency and competition

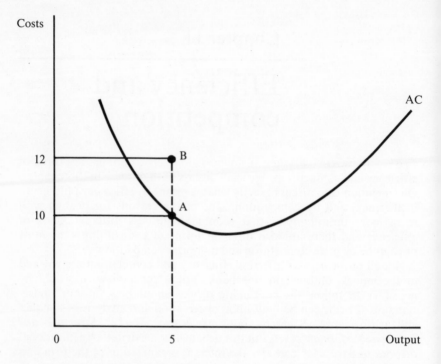

FIG. 43: Economic inefficiency in a firm

than is necessary to produce 5 units of output. Then this extra labour also contributes to costs. The firm's average cost may therefore be $12 rather than $10. Consequently, the firm is at point B and off its average cost curve. In this sense the firm is economically inefficient.

Technical efficiency and economic efficiency refer to the firm. But economists also discuss *allocative efficiency*. This is more complex and deals with the notion of whether the economy is dividing all its factors of production between firms in such a way that these firms are producing what consumers want and at the lowest possible cost. If, say, labour can be taken from one firm and put in another, leading to no loss of output in the first but an increase in output in the second, then the economy was not initially allocating its labour in the most efficient way possible. Furthermore, to be allocatively efficient requires no restriction either by the firm itself or by the government. Although in practice this is not possible, the notion of allocative efficiency provides a bench mark by which to compare different market forms.

Allocative efficiency arises from a perfectly competitive system. (Although perfect competition is not the only means of achieving allocative efficiency. It is possible to achieve the same result in a fully planned economy, but it is likely to be more difficult.) In such a system firms are perfectly competitive and they set prices equal to marginal cost. This is the crucial result in understanding allocative efficiency. If price is set equal to marginal cost then consumers are being charged at the margin what it costs the firm at the margin to produce this good. A monopolist, on the other hand, produces at an output level which equates marginal cost with marginal revenue. In this case price is above marginal cost. Consequently, consumers are being charged at a rate which exceeds the cost to the firm of producing this marginal unit.

The higher price charged by the monopolist does not indicate true scarcity relative to demand, as it would in perfect competition, but rather the fact that a monopolist can use his position to reduce output and exact a higher price. Because the price is higher, then less is demanded than it would be if the price were set equal to marginal cost. Consequently, less is produced and less factors of production are used. The economy's resources may then be inefficiently allocated.

To see why, let us compare a monopolist with a perfectly competitive firm. This is done in Fig. 44.

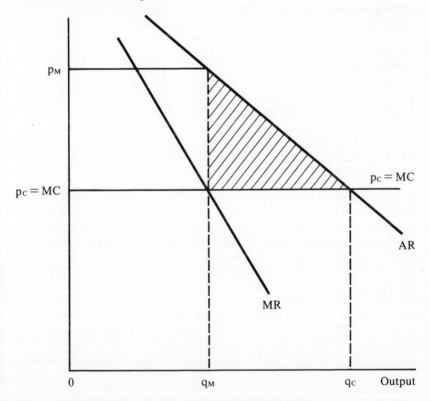

FIG. 44: **Comparison between monopoly and perfect competition**

Consider first the monopolist. In this case he sets his output where marginal cost is equal to marginal revenue. His output is therefore at q_m and his price is read off the demand curve at p_m. Notice that $p_m > MC_m$.

For perfect competition the situation is where price is equal to marginal cost equal to average cost (a long-run result of perfect competition). Thus output is q_c and price is p_c.

Two results are immediate. The perfectly competitive price, p_c, is lower than the monopoly price, p_m. Second, the perfectly competitive output, q_c, is greater than the monopoly output, q_m. The fact that, under monopoly, price exceeds marginal cost indicates that consumers are placing a high utility on the marginal unit relative to the marginal cost of supplying it. They are indicating a preference for more to be produced – more up to the point where price equals marginal cost. If this is not done then the economy is not allocating factors of production to reflect the best allocation of goods according to consumer preferences. If, on the other hand, price is less than marginal cost then consumers are indicating that too much has been produced and a better allocation is desired by moving factors of production into alternative lines of production.

The fact that price exceeds marginal cost means there is allocative inefficiency. One measure of this is the extent to which price exceeds marginal cost. The greater this difference the greater the allocative inefficiency.

Another popular measure (which is commonly used in practical studies) is the shaded area in the Fig. 44. If we take this to be approximately a triangle, then we can measure this as:

$$\tfrac{1}{2}(q_c - q_m)(p_m - MC)$$

(i.e. half the base times the height of the triangle gives its area). This measure is in monetary terms.

This common comparison between monopoly and perfect competition is misleading in one important respect. A monopolist may use his monopoly profits to undertake research and development. If this is done and is successful in lowering average and marginal costs, then the long run output level may exceed q_m (and even possibly q_c) and the price will be lower than p_m (and even possibly lower than p_c).

X-inefficiency

The concept of x-inefficiency was introduced into economics fairly recently by Harvey Leibenstein. He begins with the argument that traditional theories of the firm assume that effort is constant. In other words, managers apply themselves with a certain effort which remains constant and workers too do their jobs with always the same effort. Leibenstein argues that output can change if effort changes. Effort in turn depends on the type of contracts workers and management are involved in. If a group of workers, for instance, can negotiate better working conditions (even with the same wage) then they may increase their effort and, accordingly, the firm's output.

In a broader context Leibenstein is arguing that traditional theory always assumes firms operate at the minimum cost for any level of output. But such a notion ignores the internal workings of the firm, with its often complex internal organization. The flow of information between sections and up the hierarchical structure can be efficient or inefficient. The extent to which it is inefficient is associated with effort and this in turn depends on the type of contracts people have.

The concept is particularly useful for discussing government bureaucracies which do not produce output in the form of goods, but are usually a mechanism supplying information. Workers are often on a salary rather than a weekly wage and the only 'output' is paperwork. In these institutions there can occur *organizational slack*. The same may be true of other institutions, e.g. education and health.

Competition

Perfect competition, although assumed in much microeconomics, does not in fact exist. Certainly, unrestricted competition does not exist because of government regulations, government taxes and subsidies both on inputs and output. With many more companies being multinational it is plants (i.e. units which are parts of one firm) and not firms which exist in many countries, while the market is world-wide. Furthermore, in many countries there is a growth in the supply of information. The information industry does not have an obvious output. Information has both a quantitative and qualitative component. Because demand and supply are a mechanism to determine a market price this analysis has significance only for a monetary economy. Where barter or an informal market exists which may not use money then competition has less meaning. (An *informal economy* is where individuals mutually agree on the exchange of two goods or services usually without the medium of money and without operating through any official market – even where money is used.) A price still exists, in the sense that it is the rate of exchange, but this price tends to be locally determined in an informal economy and, more significantly, is not generally known by other market participants.

Price plays a very significant role in a market economy. It is a signal to both buyers and sellers. Too high a price will lead to excess supply and this will lead to a rise in stock levels if the good can be stored or to waste if the good is perishable. This means the price is too high and so the supplier can lower the price. Similarly, if the price is too low there will be an excess demand and supplies will be sold quickly and some customers will go unsatisfied, or stocks will be run down. This is a signal to raise the price.

It is through price that competition is considered to take place. In perfect competition the market determines the price and each firm in the industry treats this price as fixed. In other words, the firm can sell as much as it wishes at this price. It need not engage in advertising. Advertising is a means of increasing market share. But in perfect competition the firm is already selling as much as it wishes. Perfect competition also involves full information so each firm knows the same technology and exactly what other firms are doing. Even potential entrants have access to the same information. Because of this, and because the firm can sell as much as it wishes, there is no reason to engage in non-price competition, e.g. offering small goods with the purchase of so much petrol. In addition, perfect competition assumes no government restrictions of any kind (a point we shall deal with in the next chapter). In other words, perfect competition is a highly abstract notion which leads only to price competition.

Perfect competition grew out of the Darwinian view of survival of the fittest. It was thought that just as animals compete and the fittest survive, so firms compete and only the fittest survive. This biological view had already been given more economic treatment in Adam Smith's *Wealth of Nations* (1776), where the 'invisible hand' of the market mechanism allocated resources. Demand and supply would determine price and any changes, such as bad harvests or new technology, would lead to new price signals and through these a re-allocation of the economy's factors of production and new levels of output to match consumer preferences.

When we consider oligopoly, however, then many other forms of competition occur besides that of price. Price competition is still important but so too are non-price factors. Although there are many different forms which oligopoly can take, as we outlined in Chapter 9, it is still the case that non-price factors may play as important a role as price. Competition can then take the form of discounts, free goods, better after-sales service, longer guarantee periods, etc. Furthermore, quality can become an important factor. If a firm involves itself in research and development and comes up with an improved product it can lower its price, leave the price unchanged but advertise the improved quality, or even a combination of these.

It is not always the case that a market can sustain many firms and all be operating efficiently. To operate efficiently in the long run would imply a firm is operating at the minimum of its long-run average cost. In Fig. 45 we have the more likely L-shaped long-run average cost (although a U-shaped one will not affect the present argument). Market demand is given by D. Given this market demand only a few minimum efficient-scale plants are all that is required to satisfy such demand. If, for example, market demand is 30 at the minimum cost of $10, and the firm's minimum efficient scale is 15 units, then the industry can sustain only two minimum efficient-scale firms. Any more will mean each is dividing the market of 30 units and probably none will be efficient. Unit costs will then be above $10. Competition, then, is not beneficial to the consumer in this case. This example illustrates that in some high technology

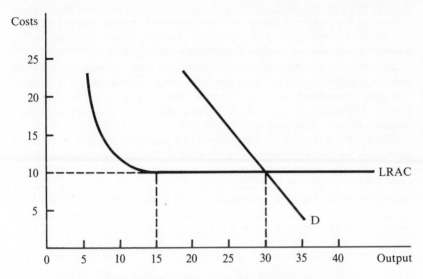

FIG 45: **Market demand and the number of minimum efficient-scale firms**

industries efficiency may require only a small number of firms. Their competition will be oligopolistic and will take the form of both price and non-price competition.

If companies become too large and show signs of becoming a monopoly then there is a tendency for governments to nationalize them. There are often common *nationalized industries* in many countries, such as transport, post, telecommunications, electricity and gas supplies. Some countries have nationalized other industries, such as steel and oil. To prevent the prospect of nationalization large companies may 'allow' smaller ones to exist to give the appearance of competition. But in these cases it is probable that the large company acts as a price leader and the small company a price follower. Competition, then, is more apparent than real.

As we move away from perfect competition it is no longer clear that firms are in fact satisfying consumer wants. Kenneth Galbraith in the United States in particular has argued that large corporations create the demand for a product. The product is made and differentiated from other products. Suppose it is 'Brand X'. The company then engages in a massive campaign to convince people that they require 'Brand X'. They accordingly create the demand for the product. With new products, too, it is not clear whether firms are supplying what consumers want, or creating those wants. In the case of video games, for instance, is there an existing demand which suppliers are simply satisfying; or, are the companies creating a demand for video games? In our modern market economy it is probably a mixture of the two. It could be argued, at least with new products, that the firm is not 'creating' demand but simply informing the public of a new commodity and all its attributes. The same argument, however, does not apply to another brand of cigarette or another brand of soap powder (i.e. not *new* commodities).

All these comments indicate that there is a close connection between efficiency and competition. Too much competition may reduce efficiency; too little competition may lead firms to take advantage of their market power. Furthermore, too much competition may lead to too little research and development.

Finally, it is not always the case that in a recession the most inefficient firms will be the ones to leave the industry. The major problem, in the short run, for a firm is cash flow. The majority of its assets are tied up in plant and machines. But in a recession interest rates tend to rise sharply. Borrowed funds are then very expensive. It is possible that a firm's flow of funds is such that it cannot even pay back the interest on a bank loan. The firms most in debt to banks are not always the inefficient firms. They usually are new firms in high risk industries.

Efficiency, competition and ecology

There is a growing view that economists have far too narrow a view of efficiency and that this narrow view, along with the concept of competition, is harmful to the country and the world's ecology. In particular, efficiency and competition leads to a rapid depletion of the world's non-renewable resources.

Non-renewable resources involve, for example, energy stored in the form of fossil fuels: coal, gas and oil. These resources have arisen over billions of years and once used cannot be renewed. Some resources are renewable, such as trees, but the major concern of environmentalists is the over-use and mis-use of different forms of energy.

Firms' costs certainly involve the costs to the firm of forms of energy. But the only costs considered are *private costs*. These are the costs borne by the firm. However, society also bears a cost in the depletion of a non-renewable resource. Such a *social cost* is ignored when considering a firm's efficiency. Consequently, an efficient production process may be highly costly to society if that process is a high energy user of non-renewable resources. Furthermore, many economies subsidize petroleum and petroleum derivatives. Because these prices are therefore low, then more is used.

Competition, as we pointed out, is a Darwinian concept arising from a biological view of a firm's behaviour. However, a more ecological view would stress the importance of systems and systems behaviour. One major feature of systems behaviour is not competition but rather co-operation. If co-operation were followed and not competition, not only would less non-renewable resources be used by present generations, but quite a different allocation of resources would result.

Chapter 12

Government involvement in markets

IN THIS CHAPTER WE INTEND TO DISCUSS the role of government and why governments intervene in the market place. There is no such thing as a totally free market mechanism. A government will tax in order to raise revenue for its various activities. Taxes and subsidies are also used as a means to improve the distribution of income – although how successful they are in doing this is very difficult to assess.

Every society possesses a government and the government not only deliberately intervenes in markets but in many it is a buyer and seller. Certainly its bureaucratic machinery employs large amounts of labour: to collect taxes, administer programmes, run nationalized industries, collect statistics, and many other activities. This collection is often referred to as the *public sector*. A concern in many countries is whether the public sector is too large and also whether it is inefficient (especially x-inefficient, as outlined in the previous chapter). This aspect of size is very much concerned with the reasons why a government involves itself in the market. An economy whose government has nationalized not only transport, gas, coal and electricity but also post and telecommunications, health, steel and oil will undoubtedly give rise to a larger public sector than one which has nationalized only transport, gas, coal and electricity, for example.

There are, then, a number of reasons why governments involve themselves in markets other than for raising revenue. They are:

(1) externalities
(2) public goods.

We shall take each of these in turn.

Externalities

First, what is an *externality*? Consider a firm which produces some chemical or other product. In doing this it requires a large cooling system which involves chimneys which give off waste products into the air. This waste is an externality. In other words, the effect is external to the firm which creates it. Consider yourself having just consumed a bottle of lemonade and you then throw the bottle away. You have also created an externality in the form of pollution (an empty bottle). Someone other than you must dispose of the bottle. In other words, the pollution you caused is external to your consumption. All pollution is an externality and the cost of it must be borne by society.

The presence of an externality gives rise to a distinction between *private cost* and *social cost*. Consider again the firm which pollutes the surrounding air. Let us suppose the firm is producing 5 million units at a total cost of $10 million. The private cost is this $10 million. But this is not all of the cost. Who pays for eliminating the pollution or the damage that the pollution causes? Let us suppose the pollution leads to damage assessed at $2 million. Then the social cost of the 5 million units is the private cost ($10 million) plus the value of the externality ($2 million), i.e. the social cost is $12 million. Notice in particular, however, that the private cost is borne by the firm while the externality is borne by society.

It is possible for a government to internalize the externality. What does this mean? In the above example the externality was valued at $2 million. Of course, this is very difficult to assess and evaluate, but we shall not discuss this here. The government could, however, tax the firm to the extent of $2 million. If it did this then the private cost would be equal to the social cost. In this case the $2 million received by the government could be used to compensate those affected by the pollution. (In practice it is not as simple as this because the tax on production will reduce output below 5 million units.)

To give one more example. Private costs of car manufacture do not cover the cost of pollution from car exhausts. The fumes from car exhausts often include lead and can give rise to lead poisoning. In large cities car exhaust fumes can increase the frequency of lung infections. These externalities show up in a larger number of people entering hospital. If the health service is nationalized then the revenue for this comes from taxation. We see, then, that car manufacturers have a private cost which is below the social cost of having that number of cars on the roads.

Governments can involve themselves in such a way as to internalize the externality and insist that a firm covers the social cost of its production. This does not mean eliminating pollution. To do so may involve not producing the good at all. What it does mean is reducing the level of output so that the loss of production which society will have to accept is just equal to the gain which society obtains from the reduced pollution. Put more technically, the marginal cost of reducing the pollution is just equal to the marginal benefit of the reduced level of pollution.

Public goods

Consider for a moment whether a single individual, no matter how rich, could pay for all of a country's defence or law and order and then recover the cost by charging people. The answer is, 'No'. If these were left to the market mechanism then they would not be provided. Society as a whole may consider them worth having but no individual is prepared to supply them. These are, then, examples of public goods. They are supplied by the government and the citizens are taxed as a means of financing them.

Another way to view a public good is that one person's consumption of it does not lessen another person's consumption. With a private good, an orange say, if I consume it then you cannot consume it. With a public good, e.g. defence and law and order, the same amount is available for everyone.

Now, although it may be obvious that defence and law are public goods, is it true of other industries the government supplies? In some countries education and health are largely run by the government. Are these public goods? The difficulty is that they have some publicness but also they can be run by private concerns. It is possible to let private individuals run all schools and charge a fee. Governments involve themselves in education and health on the grounds that a certain minimum should be available for all citizens. This does not, of course, mean complete nationalization. The problem is assessing how much.

The same difficulties may be involved in public utilities like the supply of gas, electricity and water. These could be privately supplied. However, in many highly industrialized societies this could lead to chaos if different firms were involved in supplying electricity – one digging up the road one day and another the next. Furthermore, these industries involve large-scale enterprises and their minimum-efficient scale sizes are such that just one firm only can be efficient. But even with public utilities, there is still some degree of privatization possible. Should, for instance, the distribution shops selling cookers for the gas industry or electricity industry also be run by that industry, or should they be in private hands? Similar arguments apply to transport. Although in many countries railways are nationalized there still exist privately-run bus services.

There are two observations we can make about our discussion. First, a number of industries are very expensive to operate and may be operated at a level suitable for society only if they are run by the government and not privately. Second, not all parts of the production or service need to be run by the government. Part can be run by private enterprise.

The debate, then, is not whether a government should involve itself, but rather the *degree* to which it should involve itself. This is most especially debated when considering nationalization, to which we now turn.

Nationalization

As we have just noted, one of the major reasons for nationalization of utilities – such as gas, electricity, water and transport – is that they are large-scale industries with high capital expenditure. More than one supplier would lead to excess capacity and a misallocation of resources.

Even so, such utilities are not nationalized in all countries. But when they are not, they are subject to strong government regulation.

The more usual reason for nationalization is on political grounds. If an industry becomes run down then firms will soon leave the industry. If the industry, however, is vital for the economy then one way to prevent this is for the government to nationalize it and run it at a loss. Thus, in many countries railways were first run by private firms. In this industry capital expenditure is very high. Rather than see a rapid and permanent decline in the railway systems, many governments nationalized them in order to preserve a railway network – even if it meant running them at a loss.

Similarly, in some countries governments have nationalized part or the whole of an industry which under normal circumstances would be making a loss and going out of business. The point here is that nationalization is only another way of providing a subsidy to an industry the government may wish to see continue. Whether a subsidy is better than nationalization is a difficult question to answer. It is as much political as economic. In Britain in the 1980s there is a move to return to private ownership part or the whole of some industries which had been nationalized under previous governments – a process called *privatization*.

One reason why a government may consider nationalization is to protect the public from a mis-use of power by a small group of large corporations. As we noted in our discussion of monopoly, output is smaller and price higher than under perfect competition (unless the monopolist undertakes research and development with the monopoly profits). Thus, if such a firm were nationalized then price could be lowered and output expanded.

This brings us to how a nationalized industry determines its price. If it is a public utility or even something like the railways, it is not the objective of such an industry to maximize profits. Such an objective would mean a smaller supply than that resulting from other possible objectives, and it is often the size of the industry that matters. Since efficiency in perfect competition implies price is equal to marginal cost, then it was argued in a number of countries that nationalized industries should set their price equal to marginal cost. The problem with such a rule is that it leads to an efficient allocation of resources only if all other industries are also pricing at marginal cost. Since they are not, it is not obvious that the nationalized industries should price at marginal cost.

There is a second reason why pricing at marginal cost may not be so advantageous. If the industry has a very large minimum efficient scale then it might be that average costs are falling. If this is so, then marginal cost is below average cost. To set a price equal to marginal cost would mean the industry is making a loss (since average revenue, equal to the price, is below average cost). Such a nationalized industry would need constant finance from tax receipts. One argument, therefore, is to price at long-run average cost. Put another way, the industry in the long run should break even.

What does come out of this brief discussion is that there are no clear economic arguments that would determine if and when an industry should be nationalized. Once an industry is nationalized, there is no clear rule as to how the industry should determine its output and price. It is not even clear that it is efficient for all nationalized industries to follow the *same* pricing rule.

Chapter 13

Conclusion

Limitations and extensions

The microeconomics we have outlined in this book is dependent very much on the analysis of markets. Markets are characterized by demand and supply, which together determine the price. This is true whether we are considering the price of food or whether we are considering the price of labour services. We investigated why demand curves are downward sloping and why supply curves are upward sloping. In addition we showed how taxes and subsidies affect the price and what happens when either demand shifts or supply changes.

But are prices determined by the market? Is it not the case that firms set the price and buyers just accept that price? Often when you go into a shop you do not bargain over what you pay, you accept what the price is. Although it may appear that prices are set by suppliers what matters is the effect of underlying forces which are at work. Suppose, for example, that a very high price is set. Then the supplier will not be able to sell all he would like (and if the price were very high he may not sell any at all). There would exist pressure for the firm to lower its price. The point is that as an individual you have no say in what the price is: you either buy something at that price or you do not. But the buyers as a group will reveal to the seller whether his price is too high or too low. If it is too high, in the sense that he is not selling all he would like, then he will lower the price. If his price is too low, in the sense that he sells everything he has very quickly, then he will raise the price. It is these forces which underlie market demand and supply.

But our concentration on the determination of price may give the impression that price is the most important factor when considering every commodity. This is not the case. It may be that the level of income, and the distribution of income, is more important. What matters with a number of consumer durables, like cars, television sets, washing machines, and some microelectronic equipment, is the individual's level of income. As the level of income rises in a country then there is an increase in the demand for goods other than basic necessities. As this happens, labour and capital, along with management, are switched from other goods into these which are expanding. As income expands still further these industries grow and can begin to benefit from mass production methods.

Such a move to mass production methods can be done only when demand is sufficiently high to warrant the building of large-scale plants. But once large-scale plants are built then the price of such goods will fall – as we have observed with electronic calculators and quartz watches. This will raise the demand still further. The main limitation is whether the market becomes saturated. When everyone has a car or television set then the industry can continue to expand either only if people begin to change their cars or sets more frequently, or if households begin to have more than one car or television set. Companies try to encourage more frequent changes of models in a number of ways. One is by producing goods with not too long a life. A second method is to bring out new and superior models. Much of the advertising we see, therefore, is not creating a new want but rather attracting people's attention to a new or superior model.

One of the major limitations of microeconimics is its difficulty in analysing oligopoly situations.We hinted at why this is the case in Chapter 9. Oligopoly, which is the type of market for most firms in the real world, tries to take account of one firm's behaviour on another. But human behaviour is always extremely difficult to analyse. Economists try to reduce such complex behaviour down to a few simple behaviours. For example, in the kinked demand curve theory we noted that the assumption was that if a firm raised its price then others would not follow but that if it lowered its price then other firms would do the same. This is a behavioural assumption. There are of course many others that could be made. But as the assumptions get more realistic so the analysis becomes more complex.

What we observe about microeconomics in general is that whenever it has to incorporate human behaviour then it becomes subject to criticism. In Chapter 10 we considered the labour market. This is a very complex market. In many countries the market involves the presence of trade unions. In the presence of trade unions, can we talk of the market-determined wage? In practice, bargaining is not simply about the wage but also about working conditions. This means that the analysis should incorporate the behaviour of union negotiators and the behaviour of management to such bargaining. It should be clear that this is very difficult to do, and therefore we must bear this in mind when we consider the analysis of factor markets.

One of the major limitations of microeconomics is in dealing with management and modern organizations. The firm in traditional micro-economics is an abstraction which has no existence in the real world. The manager simply makes decisions about output and price. But in the real world it is much more complex than this. The large organizations which now typify many economies are run by boards of directors who are appointed by shareholders. The organization is usually arranged into functions, such as finance, production and marketing. Decisions involve a complex interaction between the individuals of these sections of the organization. This is one of the main areas where extensions to the traditional theory are taking place. There is no basic reason why we cannot incorporate more assumptions about organization into our theories of the firm. As we have said, however, the major difficulty is that more realism usually means more complex analysis.

The government does involve itself in almost all markets. A major extension of microeconomics is in analysing exactly how governments influence decisions – especially decisions in large organizations. For instance, what is the effect of a profits tax? If labour is subsidised will firms take on extra labour? Furthermore, government-run organizations do not necessarily decide their output and price in the way that private firms do. What is needed, therefore, is analysis of private firms and a separate analysis of public corporations.

Finally, in some countries there is a development which is quite new. Some firms are owned and managed by the workers in them. Microeconomics will, in time, need to consider these developments and show whether they differ from private firms and from public corporations in their output, price and marketing decisions.

All these extensions are taking place all the time. For anyone who continues to study microeconomics, they will become the centre of that study.

Questions

1. What are the distinguishing economic features of command and market economies?

2. Examine the proposition that centrally planned economies and market economies adopt different methods to solve the same problems.

3. Comment on the ways in which variables cause changes in an individual's demand curve for a commodity.

4. Explain the meaning of
    (*a*) the price elasticity of demand, and
    (*b*) the income elasticity of demand.

   What factors determine their size?

5. What is the relationship between average revenue, marginal revenue and total revenue when demand is infinitely elastic?

6. (*a*) Explain why a distinction is made in the theory of the firm between short-run and long-run costs of production.
   (*b*) For what reason might a firm face increasing short-run marginal costs but constant long-run marginal costs for a given increase in output?

7. Define fixed and variable costs of production. What is the importance of the distinction between the two?

8. 'Under perfect competition only normal profits are earned.' Discuss.

9. Explain the price and output decision of a monopolist. What limits are there to a monopolist's power?

10. Why do firms operating in conditions of monopolistic competition have excess capacity?

11. In the short run, would you expect a firm which experienced a bigger demand for its product to
    (*a*) charge a higher price,
    (*b*) raise output, or
    (*c*) raise both output and price?

12. What factors will an oligopolistic firm have to consider when setting its prices?

13. Why is there no single theory of oligopoly?

14. What are the limitations of
    (a) mark-up pricing, and
    (b) the kinked demand theory
    as explanations of oligopoly?

15. What is economic rent and who would bear the incidence of any tax upon it?

16. To what extent does the marginal productivity theory of wages offer a valid explanation of wage levels in your society?

17. What is the meaning of 'efficiency' in economics?

18. Suppose that a perfectly competitive industry is monopolized. What will happen to the level of output of the industry and the price charged for the product?

19. Explain the difference between private and social costs of production. Show why a misallocation of resources is likely to result because of a divergence between these two costs.

20. Why do governments intervene in the market?

21. (a) What are the main reasons put forward for nationalizing industries?
    (b) Should the oil industry be nationalized?

Glossary

Cartel. A situation where a group of oligopolistic firms get together and officially agree on price and output levels.

Command economy. An economy where all decisions are made by the state.

Competition. The type of inter-relationship which exists between firms in the same industry. It can take the form of price competition or non-price competition.

Complements. Two goods are complements if they are usually used or consumed together; when the price of one goes up the demand for the other declines as a consequence.

Costs. These arise from the valuation of inputs, like labour and capital, which are used to produce output. There is a variety of costs: *total cost* is the total value of a given level of output; *average cost* of a level of output is the total cost divided by that level of output; *marginal cost* is the addition to total cost of producing one more unit of output; *fixed costs* are those costs which do not vary with output; *variable costs* are those which vary as output varies.

Cross-price elasticity of demand. This denotes the percentage change in the demand for one good arising from a percentage change in the price of a different good.

Demand curve. A curve showing how demand changes when the price changes, when all other factors like income, the price of substitute and complementary goods and tastes are held constant.

Derived demand. The demand for a factor input which occurs only because the product which uses that input (e.g. labour) is demanded.

Discriminating monopoly. A monopoly situation where the firm can sell to two or more different markets at different prices.

Distribution of income. How an economy's total income is divided between the different groups in that society.

Duopoly. An oligopoly where there are only two firms in the industry.

Economic rent. The income received over and above what a factor input is prepared to accept in payment.

Economic system. A phrase to describe all the inter-relationships of an economic nature in a country.

Economies of scale. The effect on output as a result of increasing all inputs to the same degree; e.g. if inputs are doubled and output more than doubles there are increasing returns to scale.

Efficiency. The degree to which a firm can use its technology to produce the maximum output with the minimum of factor inputs; or the production of a given output at the least possible cost; or where a country allocates its factors of production in such a way that, given all prices, there is no better way to allocate them.

Elasticity of demand. The percentage change in the quantity demanded arising from a given percentage change in the price of the same good. It is sometimes called the *own-price elasticity of demand.*

Elasticity of supply. The percentage change in quantity supplied arising from a given percentage change in the price.

Equilibrium. A state where there is a balance of forces so that there is no reason for anything to change. It is usually represented by demand and supply: where demand is one force and supply the other.

Equilibrium price. The price which arises from a balance of forces. In demand and supply it is where the two curves intersect.

Externality. A situation where an additional cost or benefit arises from consuming or producing a good for which the person consuming that good or the firm producing it does not pay for the additional cost or benefit.

Factor market. The market for a factor of production such as labour or capital.

Factors of production. An input used by firms to produce an output. These are usually grouped under three headings: land, labour and capital.

Firm. An establishment which uses factors of production to produce some output. It may be owned by the manager or owned by a group of shareholders and run by a manager.

Income elasticity of demand. The percentage change in the quantity demanded arising from a given percentage change in the level of income.

Inferior good. A good the consumption of which declines as income rises.

Informal economy. The situation where goods and services change hands and where these transactions are not officially recorded.

Input. Something used by a firm to use to produce some output. It may be a factor of production, like land or labour, or it may be the output of another firm, like steel.

Long run. A period of time which allows all the firm's inputs to vary.

Macroeconomics. The study of aggregate variables, like unemployment, inflation, interest rates, etc., and how they are all related and influence the economy.

Marginal physical product of a factor. The change in the level of output arising from a change in the level of a factor input.

Marginal revenue product of a factor. The additional value of the extra output that arises from the change in the level of a factor input.

Market. A place where buyers and sellers come together.

Market demand. The demand for a commodity which is the sum of all the individual demands.

Market economy. An economy in which individual firms and individual households make most of the decisions. Such an economy allocates goods and services by means of the market.

Market mechanism. A term used to describe demand and supply and how these interact to determine what is produced, how much and for whom.

Market price. The price of a good which is determined by the interaction of demand and supply.

Microeconomics. The study of how economies use their limited resources, such as land, labour, capital and natural resources, to satisfy the various wants of the members of that society.

Minimum efficient scale. The level of output at which the firm's average cost first becomes a minimum.

Mixed economy. An economy where households and firms make many of the decisions, but also where the state is involved in some of the decisions.

Monopolistic competition. A form of competition where the market demand curve is downward sloping and there is brand loyalty and firms use advertising to achieve it.

Monopoly. A market in which there is only one seller.

Monopoly profits. The profits of a monopolist which arise over and above normal profits.

Monopsonist. A market which involves just one buyer.

Nationalized industry. An industry which is state owned.

Normal good. A good the demand for which rises when income rises.

Normal profits. The return to management for the undertaking of combining factor inputs and taking risks. Such profits are part of the costs of a firm.

Oligopoly. A situation where there are a few firms in an industry and where each has to take account of the reactions of his competitors.

Oligopsonist. A situation where there are a few buyers and each has to take account of the reactions of other buyers.

Output. What is produced by a firm.

Own-price elasticity of demand. *See* Elasticity of demand.

Perfect competition. A form of competition where there are many sellers and none has any influence over the market price.

Physical product. The actual output arising from using factor inputs. If the total is divided by the amount of one input this denotes the *average physical product*; while the *marginal physical product* denotes the extra output from an extra unit of a given input.

Planned economy. An economy where the state takes most of the decisions on what to produce and how much to produce; and it does this usually by means of a plan.

Private costs. The costs which firms and individuals take account of in their decisions. They are to be contrasted with social costs.

Privatization. A situation where assets which have been owned by the state are sold back into private ownership.

Profits. The difference between total revenue and total cost. If this amount is positive these are sometimes referred to as *supranormal profits*. Such profits are in addition to normal profits, which are the return to management and are already part of costs.

Public good. A good which is usually supplied by the state and where one person's consumption does not limit the supply to anyone else. The usual examples are law and order and defence.

Revenue. The receipts by a firm from selling its output. *Total revenue* is the total of such receipts at each level of output; *average revenue* is total revenue divided by the level of output; and *marginal revenue* is the additional revenue that arises from an additional amount sold.

Satisficer. A firm which aims at a certain level of profits only.

Short run. A period of time where at least one factor input is held constant.

Social costs. The total cost of producing something which includes the private cost and the cost of any externality.

Subsidy. A payment to a firm which allows the firm to sell its goods at a lower price to the public. It can be a fixed amount or on every unit sold (a per unit subsidy).

Substitutes. Two goods are substitutes if the demand for one of them goes down if the price of the other goes down. If the price of meat should fall and people buy more meat and reduce the demand for fish, then meat and fish are substitutes.

Supply curve. A curve denoting how much is supplied at each price.

Supranormal profits. *See* Profits.

Tastes. The particular desires people have for certain goods and services. In demand curves these are constant, but in practice they can be influenced by advertising.

Technique of production. A particular combination of factor inputs to produce output. The same good may be capable of being produced with much labour and little capital or much capital and little labour – these are two different techniques of production.

Transfer earnings. The wage that a person or factor input would accept to move into the present situation.

Utility. The satisfaction a person derives from goods and services. Where the total satisfaction is being referred to we have *total utility*. The extra utility obtained from one extra unit consumed is referred to as *marginal utility*.

Wants. The desires people have for basics such as food, clothing and a place to live; along with other preferences for radios, TV sets, etc.

Suggestions for further reading

BREIT, W. and HOCHMAN, H. M.: *Readings in Microeconomics*, 2nd edition, Dryden Press, Hindsdale, 1971.

COHEN, K. J. and CYERT, R. M.: *Theory of the Firm*, Prentice Hall, Englewood Cliffs, 1965.

GALBRAITH, J. K.: *The Affluent Society*, Penguin Books, Harmondsworth, 1958.

GALBRAITH, J. K.: *The New Industrial State*, Penguin Books, Harmondsworth, 1967.

GALBRAITH, J. K.: *Economics and the Public Purpose*, Penguin Books, Harmondsworth, 1975.

HIRSCHLEIFER, J.: *Price Theory and Applications*, Prentice Hall, Englewood Cliffs, 2nd edition, 1980.

MANSFIELD, E.: *Microeconomics: Theory and Application*, 3rd edition, W. W. Norton, London, 1979.

MARRIS, R.: *The Economic Theory of 'Managerial' Capitalism*, Macmillan, London and New York, 1964.

SCHERER, F. M.: *Industrial Market Structure and Economic Performance*, 2nd edition, Rand McNally, Chicago, 1980.

TOWNSEND, H. (ED.): *Price Theory*, 2nd edition, Penguin Books, Harmondsworth, 1980.

Index

The author of this Handbook

RONALD SHONE was educated at the universities of Hull, Essex and Southampton during the period 1965–71. He spent five years lecturing at the University of Sheffield, and in the final stage became Esmee Fairburn Research Fellow. He moved to Stirling University in 1976 as lecturer in economics, and became Senior lecturer in 1982. His main areas of lecturing are microeconomics, macroeconomics and international monetary economics.

His previous books include: *The Pure Theory of International Trade* (1972); *Microeconomics: A Modern Treatment* (1975); *Economic Model Building* (with F. Neal) (1976); *Applications in Intermediate Microeconomics* (1981) and *Issues in Macroeconomics* (1984). He is currently working on two books: *Applications in Basic Microeconomics* (with D. N. King) and *Open Economy Macroeconomics*. He is also the author of articles on internal and external balance and the monetary approach to the balance of payments.